Endorsements

You will find a kindred spirit and radical lover of Jesus in Ashley Brendle as she transparently brings you practical, creative ways to daily walk in peace, power, intimacy, and love. Get simple, step-by-step coaching on how to connect daily and operate out of His presence. It's truly one of the greatest gifts we can give to these world changers He's entrusted to us!

Lori Byrne
Director & Vice President of Nothing Hidden Ministries,
Bethel Church, Redding, California
Author of *Love After Marriage: A Journey Into Deeper Spiritual, Emotional & Sexual Oneness*

Whether you're brand new in your Christian experience or have followed the Lord for years, Ashley Brendle's book, *Quiet Time for Busy Moms,* will refresh you with encouragement, pathways, and ideas for making your connection with God personal and clear. She leads the way to freedom from obstacles which hinder that heart to heart connection, and then lends you a hand up to that desired place.

Regina McCollam
Busy mom and church leader at The Mission, Vacaville, California
Author of *Intertwined: Strength to Stand*

If you know Ashley you have encountered her passion for and depth in God, her complete and honest vulnerability in relationship, and the authenticity with which she lives her life. Her personal journey and life in God flows across every page of *Quiet Time for Busy Moms.* Transformational truths, challenging and powerful opportunities for reflection and walking out, and an impartation to encounter God in a fresh and deeper way are waiting for you here in *Quiet Time for Busy Moms*!

Lorraine Box
Supernatural Love & Covenant Workshops, Bethel Church, Redding, California
www.SteveandLorraineBox.com

If you want to break free from the traditional idea of a "quiet time" and step into a life-giving, intimate, moment-by-moment walk with God—this is the study for you. Ashley is a living example of what it means to walk with God while keeping up with an incredibly busy family and ministry life. Her writing flows right from the lab room of her life. Ashley skillfully explores topics like breaking free from performance, attaining freedom from personal lies, the power of journaling, understanding God's goodness, how to creatively set necessary boundaries, freedom from fear, hearing God's voice and a whole lot more! Take time to enjoy and work through this study. You won't be disappointed.

Olivia Shupe
Author of *Renaissance Kids: Preparing Your Children to Thrive in a Rapidly Changing World*
www.raisingtomorrowsleaders.net

Authentic life stories, strategic insights, practical applications, Holy Spirit whispers, heart healing, and rich with extra goodies– reading this book was a joyful unwrapping of a generous gift. Thank you Ashley and Holy Spirit for showing afresh that "even in the demands of motherhood I can experience fulfillment as a daughter of God." I set this book down with an armful of truth and grace received from God encounters that were gently and skillfully directed throughout the book. My heart is overflowing in the turning of "ordinary moments into satisfying feasts." I will be returning to these pages again and again as well as sharing them with the mothers in my life.

Sarah Hatfield
Director of Agape Inner Freedom Ministries, Agape Family Fellowship, Tangent, Oregon
www.agapeinnerfreedom.org

Ashley's book *Quiet Time for Busy Moms* is a must-read. As a new mom, I felt that Ashley addressed many of the challenges I've faced in figuring out how to connect with God amidst the demands of motherhood. Her authenticity draws the reader in and puts her at ease to receive from Ashley's wisdom and life experiences. Most of all, the tools in this Bible study become like a welcome mat the reader can use to invite greater connection with God into her life.

Stefanie Overstreet
Co-Founder of Compassion to Action, Bethel Church, Redding, CA

This book is one of the best books I have read on encountering God in your quiet times. Ashley Brendle has a powerful and anointed voice for teaching mothers to break the lies of the enemy they are believing about themselves and releasing truth into their situations and into their families. What she teaches changes lives. If you want to have a deeper relationship with God, this book will give you the tools you need to do it.

Liberty Dictson
Mother of four
www.parentingmadesimple.org

Ashley Brendle's *Quiet Time for Busy Moms* has been life changing for me as I have felt the performance factor being extracted from my life with Jesus. I have been doing this performance thing a long time and so the process has been somewhat uncomfortable, but with Ashley's gentle leadership, foundation in the Word of God, and creative promptings, I can feel deep transformation rumbling inside. And I am so thankful…

Sarah Jackson
Mother of five, grandmother of two and counting

This book has equipped me to go from performance-driven devotionals to encounters with the Lord's presence! I now know how to let the Holy Spirit guide my time with Him and have been able to hear the Lord speaking to me much more clearly than ever before! My quiet time is no longer defined by crossing things off a checklist. It's about connecting with God's heart!

Shandon Gerbrandt
Mother of one

A Gift for You

Receive Your Free Set
of Quiet Time Declaration Bookmarks

Meditate on the truth of your connection with God while coloring! Tuck these cute bookmarks created just for you in your Bible or *Quiet Time* book, post them in your kitchen or on your mirror as personal reminders of God's pursuit of your heart.

Claim them today!
Go to SupernaturalMothering.com/declaration-bookmarks
Simply tell me where to send them and you'll get them in your inbox in seconds.

Thank you for reading and enjoy the journey!

Quiet Time

for Busy Moms

Break Free from Performance into Intimate Connection with God

ASHLEY BRENDLE

Dedication

*To all the busy moms trying to find Jesus
in the hustle and bustle of motherhood,
you were made for love.*

*You were born for intimate connection
with God. You are mother, but you are first
and foremost daughter of the Most High
and friend of Jesus.*

May this book help you live in His embrace.

I'm absolutely convinced that nothing—nothing living or dead, angelic or demonic, today or tomorrow, high or low, thinkable or unthinkable—absolutely nothing can get between us and God's love because of the way that Jesus our Master has embraced us.

Romans 8:38-39, MSG

Contents

introduction

My Quiet Time Dilemma

I really hate the term "quiet time."[1]

First of all, quiet is typically in short supply around a household with children. At least it is at my house. In fact, I have to get up in the wee hours of the morning in order to find it.

But there have been many times with young babies when getting up before the crack of dawn simply wasn't possible. I was too exhausted with nursing and night-wakings.

Morning would come and I'd fight to keep my eyes shut, hoping to recover a few more minutes of lost sleep. Under the covers, you would have found me praying something like, "Please God, just a few more minutes. Please don't let them wake up yet!"

Although the Lord heard and even treasured those little prayers, they don't exactly make for a quality prayer life!

Time, as well as sleep, is a precious commodity in a mother's life. There have been seasons when brushing my own teeth before I dropped into bed felt like I was pampering myself.

In my early years of raising children, time to myself seemed

---

1. Quite Time: the discipline or habitual practice of regularly reading the Bible and praying to God.

to be found only behind a locked bathroom door. Even then, there would often be little ones knocking and waiting outside. They couldn't bear any cut in communication. They would even push notes under the door.

It was like I could run, but I couldn't hide…even for five minutes. Although I tried finding refuge in the bathroom of all places, those moments never refreshed me like I had wished they would.

The changes that came with motherhood not only confronted my notions of personal space but brought a new challenge to my spiritual life as well. After my first child was born, I struggled with guilt, condemnation, and inadequacy. This, in part, was because I wasn't measuring up to the imaginary spiritual standard I had set for myself as a Christian mom.

In my mind, to be really spiritual, a one-hour quiet time was required. No matter how hard I tried, it was a rare event if I could even read my Bible uninterrupted for fifteen minutes. If I missed my quiet time, I treated it almost superstitiously and would fear I'd probably have a bad day as a result.

My quiet times were all about performance. My very sense of security and well-being depended on it. When my ability to go through all the spiritual hoops I'd set up for myself was removed, I was shaken. In motherhood, I could no longer measure up. When I was fully absorbed in motherhood with very little time to myself, my quiet times became a reminder of my shortcomings rather than of His love for me.

To be honest, even when I did have my magic formula of "quiet" and "time," I dreaded my quiet times. They felt stale and lifeless. My rigid, preconceived ideas of what spending time with Jesus looked like were holding me back from enjoying my relationship with Him.

I kept doing my quiet times out of obligation because it was the "right thing" to do. I wasn't there because of love. I mean, sure, I loved Jesus and I knew He loved me, but loving Him and receiving His love wasn't the driving motivation behind my quiet time routine.

Rather than coming as a daughter enjoying the voice and company of my Daddy, I approached Him like a slave. I was bound by the chains of fear and punishment. Deep down, I believed I must be good enough to be worthy of His love.

What About You?

Maybe your own story hasn't been quite as extreme. Perhaps your quiet times, now that you're a mother, are still a place of deep connection with God. Or maybe the idea of having a quiet time is new to you and you're reading this book without all the spiritual baggage I just described. Either way, you're ready to start cultivating a deeper relationship with Jesus.

However, perhaps motherhood has hindered your sense of quality time with Jesus and you relate to my story. Maybe you really identify with what I shared and you're worn out by the harsh taskmaster of performance and weary from the demands of motherhood. Without a life-giving way to connect and grow your relationship with God, you're frustrated, dissatisfied, and ready for a change.

Your old model of quiet time connection with God just isn't working anymore. It's true that motherhood can put limitations on the ways we can meet with God. There's little time to read the Bible, let alone study it. There's hardly time for lengthy fill-in-the-blank Bible study workbooks or intercession for the nations when the immediate needs of your family (like deciding what you're making for dinner) are constantly at the forefront of your mind.

However, the limitations that held me back from having my usual quiet time ended up being the very things that helped me break my performance-driven mold for connecting with the Lord.

Those limitations forced me to find new, intimate ways to meet God and grow connection even in the midst of busyness and the just plain craziness of motherhood. Motherhood is a gift in so many ways. For me, the gift of its challenges finally brought me to the end of myself. When I was in a place of surrender rather than pride, God was more easily able to draw me to Himself.

The principles for connecting with God in this book are not just for mothers. They can be applied to all believers in all phases of life. However, I have written this book specifically for mothers because the terrain of motherhood is special territory. I understand the demands, blessings, and concerns you face as a mom. Motherhood is a unique culture. You and I speak the same language. You're not a foreigner here. You're in good company. Your days are understood and your struggles are real. The good news is God wants to work good out of them.[2]

In this book, I'm filtering intimacy with God through this lens. Of course, you don't have to be a mom to experience deep connection with God. All the same, being a mom, sometimes you wonder if deep intimacy is still possible when there's only so much left of you and your day to go around? I believe God will use this book as a guide to show you the way.

In the following pages, I'm going to share with you how embracing the limitations of motherhood helped me break through to find new levels of intimacy with God. You'll even be empowered to set your own limits or boundaries so you can

---

2. Romans 8:28

prioritize cultivating this most valuable relationship. Even in the demands of motherhood, you can experience fulfillment as a daughter of God.

We were made for relationship with Jesus! He will bend over backwards to find ways to connect us with Himself. Won't you join me on this journey of discovering what's holding you back from deeper intimacy with God and together with Holy Spirit, strengthen your connection with Him?

How to Use This Book

This book is divided into six weeks, each full of principles as well as questions to ask yourself and Holy Spirit. I'll share with you from my own life, but Holy Spirit will make these principles fit yours. No two moms' journeys will look alike. You'll get the most out of the book when you take your time to reflect on the questions and do some of the activities. They are key to your breakthrough into a fresh perspective and deeper connection with God.

You'll want a journal to write in and record this journey. The *Quiet Time for Busy Mom's Journal*[3] is tailor-made for this particular study with headings and divisions to help facilitate your weekly progress through the book. However, any journal will do.

The *Self-Discovery Questions* are designed to help you listen to your own story and take stock of your personal journey. Asking yourself these types of questions is an essential part of your discovery process. However, they're limited to your own perspective.

The *Ask Holy Spirit Questions* get you looking upward. God values your perspective. But He wants to breathe His life-giving words on it to bring clarity and truth. This is where

---

3. Available at SupernaturalMothering.com

true freedom, healing, and breakthrough are found!

Asking Holy Spirit simply turns your prayers from a monologue into a dialogue.

Before you start working your way through the list of Ask Holy Spirit Questions, invite God to speak to you. Ask the question and then listen. You can trust Him to answer. You might hear a word, see a picture, or feel something.

It's that simple. I highly encourage you to write down the first things that come to mind when you're doing the Ask the Holy Spirit Questions.

Often, God speaks in our first impressions, before any second guessing comes into play or doubt enters in. Doubt fosters confusion and insecurity. It hinders our ability to clearly hear God's voice.

> "But when you ask, you must believe and not doubt, because the one who doubts is like a wave of the sea, blown and tossed by the wind. That person should not expect to receive anything from the Lord" (James 1:6-7).

I don't believe this verse is telling us God will punish the doubter by withholding from her. Rather, I believe we are being shown a spiritual principle: in order to receive from God, we must partner our faith with the action of coming to Him to ask. When we come, we come choosing to believe. In this way, we are acknowledging who He is, what He is capable of, and His role in our lives as a good Father.

If you get stuck or find yourself doubting what you're hearing, test your impressions with your husband or a friend. Share the question and your answer with them (if you have one). Because they know you and God's heart, they can help you discern whether what you've heard is in line with God's character and is true of you as well. If you didn't hear anything, invite them to pray, asking the question and listening with you. This is where doing the study in a small group can be particularly beneficial. God is always speaking. He wants to help us hear His voice! (Go to SupernaturalMothering. com/quiet-time-small-group-leaders-guide to access the free Leader's Guide.)

The *Pray* section encourages you to connect your heart to God's after you answer the questions. Simply use the written prayer as a starting point. Please add your own words. I want you to feel free to express your own thoughts and feelings to Jesus. You may even want to journal your prayers. Use the Scripture references to give you more understanding of the truths in the prayer.

The *Declarations* section summarizes the main truths of each week. Speak them over your life.

> "Faith comes from hearing the message..." (Romans 10:17).

Hear the truth and believe it. You may not yet be experiencing what you're declaring. But you are making a proclamation of what is to come into your life because:

> "[God's Word] will not return to me empty, but will accomplish what I desire and achieve the purpose for which I sent it" (Isaiah 55:11).

You can refer to page 129 where you'll find all the declarations gathered in one place. Also, please take advantage of my free Quiet Time Declaration Bookmarks you can color as sweet reminders of God's pursuit of your heart. (Go to SupernaturalMothering.com/declaration-bookmarks to claim them today.)

The *Step into Freedom* section will help you walk the principles out! As you do, you'll want to record your experience in your Quiet Time Journal as well. Taking action is crucial.

"You see that his faith and his actions were working together, and his faith was made complete by what he did. And the scripture was fulfilled that says, 'Abraham believed God, and it was credited to him as righteousness,' and he was called God's friend" (James 2:22-23).

As Kris Vallotton teaches, "physical obedience brings spiritual release." Your actions are an outward expression of agreement with God's truth, allowing the principles in this book to get planted more deeply into your life. The choice to take action is a powerful step that will help you live in your spiritual inheritance. Acting on revelation and faith refines and perfects its place in your life. Choose to do one or all of the suggested activities in this section. It's up to you.

Lastly, the *Journal* section prompts you to take a moment to reflect and journal what you've learned that week.

The questions have helped you evaluate your own life and invite Holy Spirit's perspective and truth. The prayer stirs your faith and initiates connection with God. The declarations are a tangible way for you to agree with God's truth and transform your mind.[4] The action steps will help you break through old habits into new ones and transform your life.

You also may enjoy adding a craft project to each week. Each craft idea was selected to inspire you to turn your weekly declarations into works of art and to help you create an expression of your intimate connection with Jesus. The suggested projects would be beautiful additions to your "secret place" (See Week Six). You'll find all the ideas and links on my Pinterest board to help you get those creative juices flowing: pinterest.com/snmothering/quiet-time-book-crafts The craft portion of the study is integrated as well into the small group study available at SupernaturalMothering.com.

---

4. Romans 12:2

Throughout the book, you'll find *Connection Points*. The purpose of this book is to deepen your connection with God. You will use some Connection Points to overcome obstacles hindering you from enjoying greater intimacy with Jesus. Others you will implement to draw you closer to God and to equip you to proactively take hold of your spiritual inheritance which Jesus died to give you!

All the connection points are strategic tools for Kingdom living. I encourage you not to leave them behind as you progress through the book. Instead, weave them into your daily life. (See page 131 for a quick reference to all the Connection Points in the book.) When you feel less connected with God, ask Holy Spirit if there is anything hindering you. Refer back to the prayers and strategies in these sections to help you or others restore connection with Jesus.

one

Redefining Your Quiet Time

Motherhood is such a major change that it requires you to adjust nearly every area of your life. As a new mother, your day is no longer your own. A little person with big needs tends to cause everything to get reprioritized. Of course, you do this with joy, but it can also cause frustration.

Everything gets redefined—how you spend time with your husband, sleeping arrangements, trips to the store, family holidays, even how you spend time with Jesus.

What doesn't change is the fact that, first and foremost, we were created to live in and desperately need intimate relationship with God regardless of the season. When we're able, we can invest more of our time into this relationship. However, there are seasons when we're just plain not able to. Even so, maintaining connection with God is vital and we can learn how to engage our heart with His no matter what our circumstances.

I believe we get stuck in feeling like we aren't being successful in our quiet times for two primary reasons:

1. We view our time with God as an obligation we are

bound to rather than a relationship to enjoy.

2. We focus more on doing rather than on being.

Our quiet time "success" doesn't rely on us. In fact, it all starts with God who is really a lover wooing us into spending time with him.

> "He is wooing you from the jaws of distress to a spacious place free from restriction, to the comfort of your table laden with choice food" (Job 36:16).

He'll free us from any obstacles and take us to the feast He's prepared. During our time with Him, he wants to fill us with His presence, hear our troubles, and calm our hearts.

> "Come to me, all you who are weary and burdened, and I will give you rest" (Matthew 11:28).

He wants to tell us secrets and show us what He's doing so we can join Him.

> "Call to me and I will answer you and tell you great and unsearchable things you do not know" (Jeremiah 33:3).

He's a proactive participant in our relationship with Him. He's always lovingly initiating connection to unite us with Himself.

He'll free us from any obstacles and take us to the feast He's prepared.

> "But whoever is united with the Lord is one with him in spirit" (1 Corinthians 6:17).

When I turned what I just described into an obligation because of my difficulty relating to God as a daughter, I lost the joy, romance, and fulfillment which He intended for me.

My focus was on meeting a requirement in my Christian

life. It was dependent on what I did: how many verses I read and how long I prayed. These superficial measurements I had set up squeezed the life out of my times with the Lord. Yet, at the same time, like the pharisees of Jesus's day, they also made me feel justified and self-righteous when I was able to achieve them.

When I became a mother and was overwhelmed with the intensity of this new season, I wasn't able to invest the time I was used to into my relationship with God.

I had limited the holy and sacred to my quiet time box.

Not only that, but I had created a restrictive box around how I defined what that time spent with Him should look like. My old mind-set insisted I meet God in my quiet times but unfortunately, I'd leave Him there. I was missing out. I had been in the habit of compartmentalizing my life. Holy and sacred here in my "quiet time box", my marriage here in my "relationship box", my hobbies in my small "free time box", my housekeeping in my "work box," etc. Living life this way was exhausting and often riddled with guilt. I felt pulled in so many directions, never managing to invest well in any of my "boxes."

I had limited the holy and sacred to my quiet time box. Without it, I wondered how I might be able to experience God. Motherhood was all-consuming. If the consistency of my quiet time was challenged, would there still be room in my life for the divine?

> "You study the scriptures diligently because you think that in them you have eternal life. These are the very scriptures that testify about me, yet you refuse to come to me to have life" (John 5:39-40).

connection point
Conſtant Connection

In the hustle and bustle of motherhood, I have connected with Jesus by:

- Praying for a situation while doing dishes at the kitchen sink
- Resting in His presence on the couch as worship music plays and kids jump from cushion to cushion[1]
- Praying in the spirit while putting laundry away
- Reading my Bible or a devotional while nursing my daughter
- Playing worship music while getting ready for our school day
- Listening to a Christian podcast while making dinner
- Reading a children's Bible while eating breakfast with my kids
- Receiving His love for me while snuggled with little ones in the early morning
- Reading a verse from the Bible open on my kitchen counter while I make the kids a snack

Did you notice every God-connection listed was lived while doing something else? The holy and sacred has found its way into my daily life, transforming ordinary moments into satisfying feasts.

Constant Connection In Action

Step 1: Try intentionally focusing on Jesus and inviting His presence into your moment.

For example, acknowledge He's near by giving Him thanks, telling Him your thoughts, or declaring His truth to your spirit. (See Connection Point: Making Declarations p. 28.) You can initiate the dialogue or simply respond to His ongoing conversation with you.

Step 2: Go about your day leaning into His words of love for you.

His Spirit makes declarations to your spirit and He sings over you with joy.[2] To lean in, spend some quiet moments listening. Or, catch His life-giving words coming to you on the fly through a friend, a podcast, the Bible, or in your head, etc.

When you do, pause. Take a deep breath. Receive the words and His love in that moment. It's a sacred one, carefully sculpted by our Father's hand to engage your heart with His.

---

1. I know that sounds crazy but at the time I was exhausted, nursing twins, and desperate for Him! Plus, my house was full of five energetic boys under the age of six.
2. Romans 8:16; Zephaniah 3:17

My Bible reading and prayer were meant to be a means to an end. Yet, they had become the end itself. I didn't know how to find security in my relationship with the Lord alone, rather than in my ritual and routine. The focus was to be relational, not ritual. The purpose of all my Bible reading and prayer was actually to lead me into personal encounters with Jesus.

Rather than just punching in my time card with Him first thing in the morning and then going about my day, I've learned to also connect with Him moment by moment. To set me free, God had to bust through the walls of my quiet time box and reclaim my heart out of the trap of performance and into the embrace of relationship.

The focus was to be relational, not ritual.

Because I'm learning to connect with Him moment by moment, my awareness of His presence throughout the day is so much greater. Every moment has become holy and sacred because He is indeed in it.

Now even the mundane tasks of motherhood like diaper changes, sorting laundry, and cleaning toilets can become potential places of encounters. Sounds crazy, right? It's simply a matter of awareness and perspective. Constant connection with God is exciting when it's about relationship, not rules!

> "For in him, we live and move and have our being" (Acts 17:28).

God is our source and everything revolves around Him and finds its fulfillment in Him. The goal is for our day, not just our quiet times, to reflect this kind of life.

Regardless of seasons and the demands on our lives, God intends us to ebb and flow with circumstances without losing our rootedness in Him.

Our ability to connect with God cannot be dependent on

quiet or time. In actuality, it's dependent on His love for each of us and the way He made for us on the cross so that we can enjoy intimacy with Him!

It's thrilling to connect with God spontaneously in all kinds of ways and places. We can find security in knowing we can access Him anytime, anywhere.

> "Let us then approach God's throne of grace with confidence, so that we may receive mercy and find grace to help us in our time of need" (Hebrews 4:16).

Our ability to connect with God cannot be dependent on quiet or time.

I like the way the Message Bible puts it: "So let's walk right up to him and get what he is so ready to give. Take the mercy, accept the help." It's always available.

In motherhood, our times of need are never ending. That's why constant connection with God is so essential so we are continually aware of the never-ending outflow of mercy and grace available for us to receive.

Self-Discovery Questions

1. What does my current quiet time look like? Describe it in detail.

2. On a scale of 1 to 10, how satisfied am I with my quiet times? (1 being totally unsatisfied and 10 being completely satisfied)

3. What do I like about my time spent with the Lord? What would I like to see change?

4. How would I like to experience my relationship with God? Write an ideal scenario.

5. How do I currently meet Jesus throughout my day, even in the busy moments?

6. What kind of season am I in? Where would I fall on the scale from intense to relaxed?

   Examples: Intense seasons require much from you (newborn baby, sickness, working part-time or full-time, etc.), whereas relaxed seasons are less demanding (more independent children, shared workload, more free time, etc.).

   intense _____ *relaxed*

Ask Holy Spirit Questions

1. How would You like to spend time with me?

2. Is there anything hindering me from experiencing deeper connection with You? (For additional help, refer to the Quick Reference: Connection Points p. 131.)

3. How would You like to meet me throughout my day? What's the feast you've prepared for me?

4. What does my current quiet time look like to You? What do You want it to look like? Ask Him for two pictures. Draw them in your journal or describe them.

Pray

"I love You Jesus. Please help me to see where You're initiating relationship with me throughout my day. Give me eyes that see and ears that hear. Increase my awareness of Your presence. I want to know You and be known by You. I welcome You to blow the lid off my quiet time box and introduce me to a relationship that pulsates with Your love for me."[1]

---

1. Psalms 139: 7-10; Jeremiah 31:3; Psalms 23:6

connection point
Making Declarations

Do you need to flip the switch in your life? Do you need a shift in your circumstances? Do you want to see something get turned around?

Declarations are a powerful force of change because they are a tool for agreeing with God's truth, and therefore, empowering it to bear good fruit in your life. We have a choice. Are we going to agree with God's thoughts and plans for our life or Satan's?

> "For as he thinks in his heart, so is he" (Proverbs 23:7, NLV).

What we think, we become. So God's word instructs us as to what to focus on.

> "Finally, believers, whatever is true, whatever is honorable and worthy of respect, whatever is right and confirmed by God's word, whatever is pure and wholesome, whatever is lovely and brings peace, whatever is admirable and of good repute; if there is any excellence, if there is anything worthy of praise, think continually on these things [center your mind on them, and implant them in your heart]" (Philippians 4:8, AMP).

We need to get in the habit of talking to ourselves. Just like David, who told his soul what to do, we need to take charge of our thought life and tell ourselves the truth.

> "Why, my soul, are you downcast? Why so disturbed within me? Put your hope in God, for I will yet praise him, my Savior and my God" (Psalms 42:5).

We can take authority and retrain our minds with what to think and what to believe. When we make declarations, we are affirming and agreeing with God's plans for our life.

Making declarations is often our initiative of "call(ing) the things that are not, as though they were" (Romans 4:17, ASV).

We get to call forth things in our lives and in the lives of others, even before we have evidence of them. It's an exciting way to co-create with God.

Declarations in Action

Step 1: Make declarations about who you are, who God is, and His promises for you.

To help, try starting your declarations with:

- I am...
- God is...
- God will...
- I can...

Step 2: Whatever lie you are confronting, use a declaration to proclaim the truth!

The truth is often the opposite of the lie coming against you.

For example, if you often feel anxious about the future, create a declaration like, "I am a woman of faith who can laugh at the days to come!"[1]

Step 3: You can always turn a Scripture verse into a declaration by personalizing it or weaving it into another declaration.

For example, take Romans 15:13, "May the God of hope fill you with all joy and peace as you trust in him, so that you may overflow with hope by the power of the Holy Spirit."

Your declaration might be, "I trust in You God. When I trust you, I am filled with all joy and peace. I then overflow with hope because nothing is impossible with God. I spill over with hope by the power of the Holy Spirit onto my kids, my husband, and my friends."

Step 4: Use the Quiet Time Declarations as starting points for your own creations or simply repeat them to grab hold of God's truth and plant it in your life.

Step 5: To remind you of the truth, creatively write your declarations on note cards, in the margins of your Bible, on signs around your home, or in your Quiet Time Journal.

---

1. Proverbs 31:25

Declarations

- I am God's precious daughter, dearly loved. I come today to spend time with Papa. It is from my connection with Him that I live and move and have my being. I position myself wide open under the spout of His mercy and grace. (Acts 17:28; Romans 8:14-16; Hebrews 4:16)

- Because of the cross, I experience constant, intimate connection with God throughout my day. Nothing can stand in the way of me living in His presence. (Romans 8:38-39; Hebrews 4:16)

Step into Freedom

Choose to do at least one this week.

BREAK OUT OF YOUR QUIET TIME BOX

Purpose to spend time with Jesus in a unique way. Try something you've never done before or haven't done in a long time. Especially consider doing something you might be inclined to think isn't all that "spiritual" (e.g., journal your prayers, sit with God in silence and even fall asleep in His arms, make a declaration, watch a movie, go for a walk, drink coffee with Him).

KEEP TRACK OF YOUR GOD-SIGHTINGS

Keep an ongoing list in your Quiet Time Journal of the unexpected ways God encounters you in the most ordinary moments and places (e.g., through an encouraging phone call from a friend, while reading a story to your kids, during a song on the radio). How is He revealing the holy and sacred of your day? At the end of the week, this list will confirm and validate His tangible presence in your life.

Journal

What did you learn? In your Quiet Time Journal, write your biggest takeaway from this week.

two

Tending the Garden of Your Heart

I don't have much of a green thumb. In fact, I'm only fairly successful keeping succulents alive. That's because succulents only have to be watered about once a week. They are low-maintenance plants. With my high-maintenance family of eight kids, succulents are about all I can handle. However, there's some gardening I can't ever consider optional—it's the gardening of my heart.

Even in the most difficult times and challenging circumstances, each of us is responsible for tending the garden of our heart. We each must take care of our own spiritual health. Each person's relationship with God is her own responsibility and no one else's.

This is actually good news. It means we're powerful to choose Him in all things, at all times. However, choosing Him can be more easily said than done.

Because of the unending needs we tend to in a home with children, it's all too easy to find ourselves at the bottom of our own to-do list. I used to think this kind of martyrdom was a non-negotiable part of motherhood.

I believe in serving my kids and being willing to die to myself. Unfortunately, like many moms, I embraced these to an unhealthy extreme. My perspective on always putting my own needs last radically shifted after reading *Loving Our Kids on Purpose* by Danny Silk.

> *It's all too easy to find ourselves at the bottom of our own to-do list*

"Taking good care of our children begins with learning to take care of ourselves. . . . If you don't take care of yourself, you won't last long trying to take care of another person. You have to have a high value for taking good care of you! Somewhere along the road, somebody taught us that a worn-out, burnt-out, frustrated, bitter parent is a good one. Somehow that's holy and noble."[1]

That's exactly what the martyr philosophy of motherhood produces. So rather than submitting to this, we can choose to take care of ourselves. One way to do this is prioritizing spending time and energy investing in our relationship with God. When we put our relationship with God first, we will thrive!

Your Choices are Powerful Guardrails in Your Life

Danny Silk says, "Boundaries communicate value for what is inside of those boundaries."

When you set healthy boundaries to get your own needs met, you are valuing the well-being of your heart. Your kids actually learn to value what is inside of them as you, their mother, demonstrate value for what's inside of you.

We are powerful to choose. In fact, I've heard it said that in not choosing, we're really choosing. There's always a choice to be made.

---

1. Danny Silk, *Loving Our Kids on Purpose: Making Heart to Heart Connection*, 2013.

Other people, who want something from us, are more than happy to make that choice for us. If we aren't assertive about the priorities of our life, those people will choose for us and often, their choice is not in line with what we value. Not because they're mean and vicious, but simply because we're not protecting and guarding what's important to us.

One summer, I served as a snack helper at our church's Vacation Bible School program. We had a nanny who cared for my kids three hours a day. We were working through the schedule for the week of VBS when she shared she was not going to be available to switch her hours to accommodate my volunteering at church that week.

My heart sank. I would not have the freedom that week to run errands and grocery shop without all my little ones nor would I be able to invest the same amount of time in my ministry. Her choice to stick to our predetermined schedule felt unfair. Why couldn't she be more cooperative?

I quickly caught myself in my unhealthy thought process. I wasn't a victim to my nanny's choices. I was powerful to make choices too. I had chosen to serve at my church and participate in a program alongside my kids. This was fun and would give me joy.

Instead of feeling someone was taking from the time I normally devoted to my ministry and errands, I *I determined to own my choice and the sacrifices that went with it* realized I was just making a different choice that week. It was still a good one. It was a choice to invest in my church, community and most importantly, in building memories with my kids.

So, I determined to own my choice and the sacrifices that

went with it. I committed not to make it anyone else's fault or problem when I grocery shopped with kids in tow or woke up early to squeeze some writing in. I would do it with joy. For it was my choice and that makes me powerful!

I was exercising my power to choose my priorities and protect what I valued. I had been afraid I was putting my own needs on the back burner again. Rather than putting someone else's needs before my own, I was simply choosing to focus on a different need of my heart that week.

Boundaries function like guardrails in your life. They keep you on course and help ensure you move in the direction you desire. You can't thrive without them. Your "no" to one thing makes way for your "yes" to another. In order to be able to do this with confidence, we must take time to listen to our own needs and to Holy Spirit.

Cherie Bolz says, "Your choices today will define your road and your journey tomorrow."

Boundaries help you live purposefully. In motherhood, it's all too easy to allow our days to get swept up in the current of urgency around us. We start going along with the crowd (which often consists of our children) and live our days as victims to all their needs and desires.

Your "no" to one thing makes way for your "yes" to another

With Holy Spirit, you can take charge of your day and put guardrails in place that make room for you to take care of your own heart. These guardrails can be big or small.

Sometimes it may look like an afternoon or weekend away, doing as you choose. Other times, it may simply be saying no to a child's interruption to a conversation or an earlier bedtime for them to protect what's important to you. Currently, how I organize my schedule serves as the most significant guardrail in my life.

The Lord may direct you to draw emotional or physical boundary lines to protect the garden of your heart. As Danny Silk illustrates, these may look like a deer fence or just some chicken wire depending on the "opportunivores" in your habitat.[2]

God doesn't call us to work tirelessly from sunup to sundown without taking time to tend the garden of our heart. Connecting with God and what is going on in our own heart will allow us to live wholly and fully alive in all circumstances.

The Value of "Thinning Out" Your Life

One summer, while we were missionaries in Corsica, France, I dared to plant a vegetable garden. I was a novice gardener and had a toddler so I had my work cut out for me. We planted rows of juicy beefsteak tomatoes for caprese salad, far-reaching zucchini plants for their blossoms dipped in batter and deep-fried, and green, bushy cilantro to use in my homemade salsa. Tending these vegetable plants was rewarding, but then, there was my carrot patch.

I planted my carrots from seed and carefully read the package to ensure their success. However, I did not like what I read. It told me to thin the carrots when their green tops were four inches tall.

Everything in me was absolutely against this advice. Why would I pluck perfectly good carrots out of the ground in their infancy? After all, I wasn't sweating and toiling for nothing. I was after a big harvest.

So I refused to do it.

Later in the summer, when it came time to gather my

---

2. Danny Silk, *Loving Our Kids on Purpose: Making Heart to Heart Connection*, 2013.

carrots, I learned the hard way why it would have paid off to have listened to the counsel on the seed packet. Instead of long, firm carrots reaching far down into the soil, I pulled up stubs about two inches long.

Thinning out your life takes faith My carrot seeds had needed more room to grow so they didn't have to compete with their neighbors for nutrients, moisture, and light.[3] When I scattered the seed, they were naturally too close together. Thinning them out would have allowed for those that remained to grow to full maturity. That summer, all I harvested were baby carrots.

No, they didn't go to waste. I cooked them and declared them *"carottes vichy,"* a French dish of softened, buttery carrots. However, I was disappointed.

When I became pregnant with our eighth baby, God reminded me of this experience as I was whining about how this unexpected pregnancy was postponing some other plans I had made for my future.

He was asking me to "thin out" my day and the next nine months so what was already planted within me could run its course to full maturity. My daughter and a move from Alaska to California took over my garden. With God's wisdom, I cut our homeschooling year a few months short, pulled out extra-curricular activities, and put my blog on hold.

It was hard to pull out areas of my life that had the potential to bear fruit. Yet, I knew God was warning me that if I let everything remain planted in my garden, I risked an underdeveloped harvest.

Thinning out your life takes faith.

Had I tried to do everything I might have faced exhaustion, frustration, disappointment, and half-hearted attempts

3. cedarcirclefarm.org/tips/entry/how-to-thin-carrots

to keep it all going. God was looking out for the harvest of my heart. He didn't want me to experience devastation, but a simplified life in full bloom.

> "The thief comes only to steal and kill and destroy; I have come that they may have life, and have it to the full" (John 10:10).

When God leads us to thin out our life, it is often a timely request and for good reasons.

> "Every branch that does bear fruit he prunes so that it will be even more fruitful" (John 15:2).

He wants us to bear lots of fruit. He tends our lives and our hearts in such a way that will produce to the max if we are willing to listen and obey His wisdom and step into His grace.

He didn't want me to experience devastation, but a simplified life in full bloom

It's the grace to lay things aside, to refocus, to slow down. Be assured. If God asks you to do it, He will give you the grace you need to carry it out.

Winning in God's Kingdom

In the early hours one morning, before anyone else was awake, I sat at my writing desk spending time with Jesus. Joseph (then age five) quietly entered and curled up in the rocking chair next to my desk.

My mama heart loved seeing him snuggled there with a blanket next to me. However, I knew I desperately needed this quiet, personal time to be able to pour my heart out to Jesus.

I was torn between my own needs to connect with God and the needs of Joseph to connect with me.

But I chose.

I gently told him this was my time to meet with Jesus. I gave him a couple choices of where he could go and what he could do in the meantime. Then, I told him we'd make breakfast together soon.

This is an example of a boundary I set to protect my garden. It was small. However, it was really significant for me. I was able to prioritize my connection with God while maintaining my connection with my son.

I was able to prioritize my connection with God while maintaining my connection with my son

Through my choice that morning, I was able to teach Joseph my relationship with Jesus is important and therefore, his relationship with Jesus is important too and worth guarding like a treasure. Now those are lessons I want him to learn. I was able to teach him as I chose to take care of myself. Amazing!

We often view prioritizing our own needs in terms of winning and losing. We think, "If I focus on getting my own needs met, I win, but that means somebody else loses."

Not in God's Kingdom. He is all about win-win! He wants us to order our life according to His life-giving principles in the Word and then simply trust Him.

We might be hesitant to do this because we're afraid someone else, namely our husband or kids, will lose if we do.

But if you "seek first his kingdom and his righteousness… all these things will be given to you as well" (Matthew 6:33). Here's the win-win!

We can trust Him to show us ways to take good care of ourselves spiritually, emotionally, and physically that will at the same time empower us to better care for those around us.

Drawing Spiritual Boundary Lines

Boundaries help us keep the bad out so the good we're cultivating inside the boundary lines thrives.

> "The boundary lines have fallen for me in pleasant places;
> surely I have a delightful inheritance" (Psalms 16:6).

Another word for inheritance is legacy, which means "anything handed down from the past."[4]

These God-directed boundary lines help ensure what gets handed down to us from previous generations and from our own past is indeed delightful. By the blood of Jesus, you have authority to draw spiritual boundary lines through the power of the cross.

Recently, I was spending time with an extended family member and was receiving mixed messages about the gifts she was giving me. I could tell she really wanted to be generous with me but there was always something holding her back. In fact, she had even given me something and then out of fear of not having it herself, she took it back (after I offered it to her having seen her hesitation).

I felt hurt and confused. I prayed and poured out my pain and even anger to Jesus. He

By the blood of Jesus, you have authority to draw spiritual boundary lines through the power of the cross

helped me discern this person was under a spirit of poverty. That was the yuck I was experiencing.

Immediately, I prayed a prayer to affirm my spiritual separation from this generational baggage that was encroaching on the garden of my heart. I also repented of any ways I had personally agreed with poverty in my own life.

---

4. Legacy. Dictionary.com

In addition, I forgave her for partnering with the spirit of poverty. I prayed, "Help me be generous when it's in my power to be so."

When opportunities arose to give a little extra or offer something I had to spare, I proactively agreed with my actions that I am free from poverty and therefore I have more than enough from which to give!

The cross is the most powerful boundary God has ever established. He put it between us and the kingdom of darkness. In

The cross is the most powerful boundary God has ever established

lifting Jesus up on the cross, God proclaimed, "Sin stops here! Curses end! Sickness is finished! Death reigns no more!"[5] On the other side of the cross is Jesus's abundant resurrection life.

The cross of Jesus becomes the spiritual boundary between our old life and our new life in Him. Sometimes the enemy tries to drag us back and convince us we are powerless and destined to live a life trapped in our old, familiar inheritance.

This is a lie. The cross of Jesus is a vivid display of God's victory and our promised land. We get to choose which side of the cross we will live on.

> "But you will cross the Jordan and settle in the land the Lord your God is giving you as an inheritance, and he will give you rest from all your enemies around you so that you will live in safety" (Deuteronomy 12:10).

Just as with the Israelites, there are necessary battles to fight as we settle in our promised land. We must be prepared to take up our spiritual weapons and tear down any strongholds in our life. In this way, we lay hold of our spiritual inheritance.

God empowers us to silence the liars in our lives so that

---

5. Isaiah 53:5; Galatians 3:13

connection point
Freedom from Generational Sin

Have you ever experienced an interaction with a family member where you could feel "yuck" coming against you but perhaps you couldn't specifically define what it was? You may not have brought it with you into the room, but it's being thrown your way. When we've been in the rut with someone else's unhealthy habits of interaction, the yuck can feel all too familiar.

Or perhaps you've dealt with fear, a poverty mind-set, discouragement, or depression (to name a few) that continually plagues you and you recognize a family member similarly struggling with this same issue?

By taking these six steps, you will experience freedom, deliverance, and your Godly inheritance bought for you by the blood of Jesus.

When I first take ground back from the enemy, I might have to repeat these steps several times a day. Repeating the process doesn't mean it hasn't worked.

> "Submit yourselves, then, to God. Resist the devil, and he will flee from you" (James 4:7).

It's our way of submitting to God and resisting the devil. One offensive strategy against the enemy is to stand on the finished work of the cross. The prayer process below will empower you to stand on what Jesus did. Repeating it is your way to keep standing!

> "Be prepared. You're up against far more than you can handle on your own. Take all the help you can get, every weapon God has issued, so that when it's all over but the shouting you'll still be on your feet" (Ephesians 6:13, MSG).

Freedom from Generational Sin in Action

Step 1: Complete the following exercise in your journal.

In your journal, draw the cross of Jesus, representing the line between your old inheritance through your natural family line and the new inheritance you have through Jesus. List the parts of your old inheritance you'd like to lay down and exchange on one side of the cross. On the other side, write what you gain by the blood of Jesus.

> "Therefore, if anyone is in Christ, the new creation has come: The old has gone, the new is here!" (2 Corinthians 5:17).

Step 2: Break free from any generational sin.

Pray: "I put the cross of Jesus between me and my bloodline, a thousand generations back and a thousand generations forward. By the blood of Jesus, I am free from ____ (name the "yuck" (sin) coming against you or ask Holy Spirit to show you exactly what it is). Because of the cross, ____ (name the "yuck") no longer has authority in my life."[1]

Step 3: Take responsibility for any ways you've agreed with this sin in your own life (See Connection Point: Repentance p. 44.)

Pray: "I repent from agreeing with ____ (name the "yuck") in any way. I receive Your forgivenesses for my sin."

Step 4: Forgive the family member whose partnership with the yuck has negatively affected you (See Connection Point: Forgiveness p. 47.)

Pray: "I forgive ____ (name the family member) for partnering with ____ (name the "yuck") and I release him/her to you and ask that you bless him/her."

Step 5: Ask God to empower you to live out of your new inheritance (which is often the opposite of what has been coming against you).

For example, instead of poverty, I asked Him to help me be generous and believe I have more than enough (See Connection Point: Exchanging Lies for Truth p. 71).

Pray: "Holy Spirit, please remind me of my deliverance made complete for me on the cross and empower me to say 'no' to receiving ____(name the "yuck") again and 'yes' to receiving ____(name your Godly inheritance)."

Step 6: Act on it.

For example, I began looking for ways to proactively be generous in order agree with my deliverance from poverty and my new inheritance of generosity.

1. Byrne, Barry, and Lori Byrne, *Love After Marriage: A Journey into Deeper Spiritual, Emotional and Physical Oneness*, 2009.

we may rest in complete safety from the enemies around us.[6] He has given us authority to protect the fruit of His Spirit in our hearts by wielding the sword of the Spirit, the word of God (His truth) in the enemy's face. (See Connection Point: Exchanging Lies for Truth p. 71.)

"For though we live in the world, we do not wage war as the world does. The weapons we fight with are not the

6. Psalms 63:11; Hebrews 4:3

weapons of the world. On the contrary, they have divine power to demolish strongholds" (2 Corinthians 10:3-4).

The boundary lines have fallen for you in pleasant places. God has drawn them with the cross.

Step into your place of authority and break free from strongholds in your natural inheritance so you can fully enjoy your promised land.

Our heart is the source out of which our everyday life flows

Jesus, The Master Gardener

When I don't take time to connect with God for a few days, the results aren't pretty.

In fact, they're just plain ugly. I easily become governed by fear, frustration, and weariness rather than the fruit of the infilling of His Spirit.[7] It's because I'm continually pouring out without constantly being filled up. Neglecting to tend the garden of my own heart is too costly on me, my husband, and my children.

> "Above all else, guard your heart, for everything you do flows from it" (Proverbs 4:23).

Our heart is the source out of which our everyday life flows. Jesus promised us,

Our part is to believe. God's part is to fill us and flow through us

> "'Whoever believes in me, as scripture has said, rivers of living water will flow from within them.' By this he meant the Spirit, whom those who believed in him were later to receive" (John 7:38-39).

Simply believing in Jesus releases this spring of living water

---

7. Galatians 5:22

connection point
Repentance

When we recognize sin in our life, we must radically uproot it. Sin separates us from God and hinders our intimate connection with Him. That is why these weeds in our garden are so deadly. It is the cross of Jesus which gives us power through Holy Spirit to repent, or turn away from sin.

To repent means "to change one's mind and purpose."[1]

"It is important to repent to something, not just from something. It involves changing the mind from one course into a higher course."[2]

You were headed in one direction when you believed the lies of the enemy, which led you into sin. Since repentance involves changing your mind, when Holy Spirit convicts you of sin, He wants you to first stop thinking the enemy's thoughts so you can start thinking His thoughts.

The truth puts you on a different course. You are now positioned towards God's purpose. Your new thoughts have set you up to reap godly results, a righteous life.

> "If we confess our sins, he is faithful and just and will forgive us our sins and purify us from all unrighteousness" (1 John 1:9).

Repentance In Action

Step 1: Ask Jesus for forgiveness.

Pray: "Jesus, please forgive me for partnering with ____(name the sin). Wash me with your blood. I turn away from the plans that ____(name the sin) had for the direction of my life and heart."

Step 2: Exchange the sin for God's blessing.

The cross of Jesus is the place of this great exchange.

Ask: "What do You have for me instead?" Listen.

If you're having trouble hearing, Holy Spirit often wants to give you the opposite of the weapon sin has formed against you.

For example, instead of bitterness, God may want to give you forgiveness. This would lead you to also pray the prayer under Connection Point: Forgiveness p. 47. Or, instead of envy, God may want to give you contentment.

---

1. *Dictionary of Words from the King James Bible*, 1999.
2. Steve Backlund, *Igniting Faith in 40 Days: The Power of Declarations and Negativity Fasts*, 2012, p.19.

Step 3: Thank God for what He's done.

Pray: "Thank You Jesus for forgiving me and making my heart clean. Thank you for the gift of (name what He gave you instead). I turn towards (name the gift) instead and choose Your path of righteousness."

For example, envy leads to a joyless life. When I receive and agree with God's contentment, I'm headed in a better direction. It puts me on the pathway of thankfulness, joy, and peace instead.

Step 4: Commit to righteousness.

After you've acknowledged your sin, confessed, and received the gift and new mind-set towards it, you need a plan. Especially when we've struggled with a habitual sin, we set ourselves up for failure if we don't have a Holy Spirit strategy for success.

Pray: "Holy Spirit, empower me to walk out my repentance. What system can I put into place or step can I take that will act like fly paper to catch the lies that are driving me and take them captive?"

For example, in my tendency to strive, whenever I start trying to achieve things in my own strength, I can commit to stop what I'm doing and search my heart. When I do, I might realize what is cracking the whip behind me–fear of failure and fear of lack. So, I'll repent again of believing the false promises they are making to my identity. I will turn from striving to a trusting, dependent relationship with my Heavenly Papa.

Step 5: Make a declaration.

For example, in the above scenario, I could use Scripture like Psalms 20:6-7,

> "Now this I know: The Lord gives victory to his anointed. He answers [her] from his heavenly sanctuary with the victorious power of his right hand. Some trust in chariots and some in horses, but we trust in the name of the Lord our God."

I can also boil the six step process down to a single statement that reminds me of my repentance. (See Connection Point: Making Declarations p. 28.)

(Holy Spirit) within us. (See Connection Point: Baptism of the Holy Spirit p. 64.)

Our part is to believe. God's part is to fill us and flow through us. Sound simple enough? So, why don't we continually experience the rivers of living water flowing from our heart? Why does it sometimes feel like a little trickle?

The living water can get clogged by our unbelief and sin.

These weeds inhibit the life of the Spirit we are desiring to cultivate, making the harvest of our heart less fruitful. Jesus, our Master Gardner, wants to help us weed the garden of our heart.

Potential Weeds

BLAME, RESENTMENT & BITTERNESS

When I don't take responsibility for my own choices, I see myself as a victim of my circumstances. Or, when I harbor offense and unforgiveness towards someone, my heart hardens. It becomes a breeding ground for blame, resentment, and bitterness to grow up.

> "And do not grieve the Holy Spirit of God, with whom you were sealed for the day of redemption. Get rid of all bitterness, rage and anger, brawling and slander, along with every form of malice" (Ephesians 4:30-31).

How do we get rid of blame, bitterness, and resentment? We must recognize and own our partnership with them and repent. (See Connection Point: Repentance p. 44.)

UNFORGIVENESS

Read Matthew 18:22-35 to get some context for the following verse.

> "In anger his master handed him over to the jailers to be tortured, until he should pay back all he owed. 'This is how my heavenly Father will treat each of you unless you forgive your brother or sister from your heart'" (Matthew 18:34-35).

At first, these can be hard Scriptures to swallow. Yet, they are actually steeped in so much grace for ourselves and for those who have sinned against us.

connection point
Forgiveness

It is humanly impossible to forgive on our own. However, we don't forgive in our own strength. It's only through the power of Holy Spirit that we can obey this command and walk it out.

This three-part prayer is a powerful expression of the finished work of forgiveness. It helps us totally surrender our situation to God and aligns us with His heart for ourself and others.

Forgiveness in Action

Pray: "Jesus, I forgive _____(name the person) for _____(name the offense). I release him/her to You and I ask You to bless him/her."

Step 1: Choose to forgive.

It's an act of obedience.

> "...forgiving each other, just as in Christ God forgave you" (Ephesians 4:32).

Step 2: Release the person to Jesus.

In doing so, you renounce your role as judge over the person's life. We may desire justice. Rest assured. Justice has been done because all sin is covered by the blood of Jesus.

> "And he has given him authority to judge because he is the Son of Man" (John 5:27).

However, because of the work of the cross, Jesus says,

> "I did not come to judge the world, but to save the world" (John 12:47).

Step 3: Ask God to bless them.

Praying this portion of the prayer is often the most difficult for me. I want justice, restitution, and reconciliation. However, it does release His promise that

> "...God's kindness is intended to lead you to repentance" (Romans 2:4).

Forgiving, releasing, and agreeing with God's desire to bless the person will open the pathway for repentance and an about-face change in the offender's life, as well as God's grace to flow into their life and yours.

When I've stood in judgment and unforgiveness towards others, I've tangibly experienced the "torture" of the demonic in the night hours. For years, I battled it without knowing I had opened myself up to this because of my unwillingness to

connection point
Thanksgiving & Praise

When I'm feeling distant from God, I give thanks. Not for the distance, but because thanksgiving is a doorway into His presence.

> "Enter his gates with a song of thanksgiving and his courts with praise. Be thankful to him, and bless and praise his name" (Psalm 100:4).

Thanksgiving welcomes God's presence and shifts the atmosphere of discouragement and despair over your life! He invites you to trade in a spirit of despair for a garment of praise (Isaiah 61:3). Thanksgiving also connects us to his goodness.

Thanksgiving & Praise in Action

Pray: "Thank You Jesus for ____(name five to ten things you are thankful for. Think about what God has done and what He is able to do). I praise You Jesus because you are ____(name five to ten qualities and characteristics you love about Him)."

forgive. I wasn't consciously being unforgiving.

However, after some counseling, I was able to admit the hate hidden in my heart and repent of my unforgiveness. As I began to work through my own grief and chose to forgive, the demonic presence left.

Harboring unforgiveness in our hearts locks us in a prison of our past

"In prayer there is a connection between what God does and what you do. You can't get forgiveness from God, for instance, without also forgiving others. If you refuse to do your part, you cut yourself off from God's part" (Matthew 6:15, MSG).

Without doing our part, we hinder what God wants to do in our lives and the lives of our "offenders." Harboring unforgiveness in our hearts locks us in a prison of our past.

If we refuse to forgive, we keep ourselves from moving out of the past into the grace available to us in the present. The reality is forgiveness not only sets the "offender" free, but it sets us free as well. (See Connection Point: Forgiveness p. 47.)

CRITICISM & NEGATIVE THINKING

Our words and thoughts can muck up the river that flows from our heart. Before we know it, stinkin' thinkin' can lead us down the path of judgment, jealousy, and even hate.

> "Out of the same mouth come praise and cursing. My brothers and sisters, this should not be. Can both fresh water and salt water flow from the same spring?" (James 3:10-11).

Our words can either produce life or death. Our tongue is a weapon. We can use it for good or for evil.

> "Death and life are in the power of the tongue, and those who love it and indulge it will eat its fruit and bear the consequences of their words" (Proverbs 18:21, AMP).

If you find yourself feasting on critical and negative thoughts and words, stop right now and repent to break the cycle. (See Connection Point: Repentance p. 44.)

Our words can either produce life or death

Instead of the ill-fitting clothes of negativity, put on the beautifying garment of praise and thanksgiving.[8] When you want to spew criticism, reject the temptation and begin praising God for who He is and thanking Him for what He's done and what He will do![9] (See Connection Point: Thanksgiving & Praise p. 48.)

---

8. Isaiah 61:3
9. I'm not advocating living in denial about difficult circumstances. Instead, I'm encouraging honesty while partnering with God's life-giving plans for the situation by speaking life over it rather than death.

As you tend the private garden of your heart, put up fences, pull up weeds, and thin out patches, the description in the passage below will be true of you.

"For I find the Promised Land flowing within you. The fragrance of your worshiping love surrounds you with scented robes of white. My darling bride, my private paradise, fastened to my heart. A secret spring are you that no one else can have—my bubbling fountain hidden from public view. What a perfect partner to me, now that I have you. Your inward life is now sprouting, bringing forth fruit. What a beautiful paradise unfolds within you" (Song of Songs 4:11-13, TPT).

Self-Discovery Questions

1. On a scale of 1 to 10, how well am I taking care of myself? (1 being neglectful and 10 being extremely attentive)

2. How do I feel when I do something for myself? (relieved, refreshed, guilty, regretful, etc.)

3. On a scale of 1 to 10, how often do I choose to put my kids' needs before my own? How satisfied am I with this current ratio? (1 being always putting my kids' needs first and 10 being always putting my own needs first)

4. Have I neglected any areas in the garden of my heart where weeds have tried to hinder new growth? If yes, list the weeds.

Ask Holy Spirit Questions

1. How do You view and value my needs?

2. What does the garden of my heart look like to You? Ask Him for a picture. Draw it in your journal or describe it.

3. How do You view and value the needs of my children? Please give me a picture of how to balance my needs and their needs in my daily life. Draw it in your journal or describe it.

4. Are there any new guardrails I need to put up to guard what I value and the direction of my life? If yes, which ones? What can I do?

5. Are there any areas of my life that would be more fruitful if I thinned them out? If yes, which ones? What can I stop doing so that I have more room to grow what's important to me and You?

6. Do I need to draw any spiritual boundary lines? If yes, use the Connection Point: Freedom from Generational Sin p. 41.

7. If you made note of any neglected areas of your heart in Self-Discovery Question number four, ask: What do I need to do to weed this area of my heart? You can use the Quick Reference: Connection Points p. 131 as your gardening tools.

Pray

"I receive Your permission to value and take great care of myself. I thank You for faithfully caring for my needs and the needs of my husband and children as well. I trust You to show me how to maintain a loving connection with my children, even while I choose to invest in my own needs. With Your help, I choose to prioritize cultivating the garden of my heart and my relationship with You."[1]

---

1. Song of Songs 4:12; John 15: 1-8; 1 Peter 5:7

Declarations

- God shows me creative ways to establish the necessary boundaries to tend the garden of my heart and prioritize spending time connecting with Him.[2]

- I guard my heart and the fruit of the Spirit blossoms in it![3]

Step into Freedom

Choose to do at least one this week.

TAKE CARE OF YOURSELF

Choose one way to take care of yourself this week and make it happen! (Curl your hair, say no to a request that conflicts with your own needs, shower [c'mon mamas of new babies, I know how that goes!], paint your toenails, exercise, etc.)

PUT ON YOUR GARDENING GLOVES

After answering the above questions, you may have discovered areas in your heart you've neglected. No worries! This is what tending your garden is all about. It's a part of a healthy spiritual life.

This week, spend time focusing on one area Holy Spirit showed you. What will you do that will bring you closer to your goal of a well-tended heart? (Forgive, dream, hope, laugh, etc.) Make a commitment and write it in your journal as a gentle reminder to yourself this week.

Journal

What did you learn? In your Quiet Time Journal, write which truth impacted you the most this week.

---

2. Psalms 16:6; Revelation 2:4
3. Proverbs 4:23; Galatians 5:22-23

three

Freedom from the Performance Trap

Before I began confronting the hold performance had on my life, focusing on the tasks of my quiet time was the driving and all-consuming force behind my time with God. I'd approach God attempting to do all the "right" things in order to secure my relationship with Him. I'd leave my quiet time having checked off my list of prayer points and Bible reading without really experiencing what I so desperately needed—God's love and presence.

Larry Randolph says, "Life in God is not about our push or our performance, it is about His presence."[1] Boy, had I missed the boat!

I did want His presence. I knew I'd just been going through the motions.

"Religion is based on what we do for God and Christianity is based on what He has done for us. Religion works *for* love,

---

1. Olivia Shupe, *Renaissance Kids: Preparing Your Children to Thrive in a Rapidly Changing World*, 2012.

while Christianity works *from* love and relationship" (emphasis mine).[2]

It was clear; I was working for love. I had been hung up on religion, not true Christianity. Yet, I didn't know how to do relationship with God any other way. So, how did I get here? Why did I find myself caught in this trap of performance which prevented me from experiencing the intimacy with God I really craved?

Looking for Love in All the Wrong Places

In my case, it was some wounds from my childhood that had produced this endless drive within me for security through performance. After my parents divorced when I was four, I feared rejection.

I began believing the lie that if I was good enough, I could protect myself from ever experiencing rejection again. If I was good enough, then I'd be worthy of love. I tried hiding my true self (the not-so-good-enough self), under layers of performance, never risking exposing her to rejection.

The flip side of this coping mechanism was that I could never let myself be truly known, not even by God. I was struggling to let the raw and vulnerable places in me come out into His light. Growing up, I hadn't experienced a safe place to really let my guard down and be vulnerable. As a result, I was afraid to get too close, to let myself be truly embraced.

On God's terms, spending time with Him is meant to be a living, fluid relationship filled with intimate conversations

---

2. Olivia Shupe, *Renaissance Kids: Preparing Your Children to Thrive in a Rapidly Changing World*, 2012.

So, I became self-sufficient in regard to my own needs, even if it meant I had to manipulate and control things to get what I wanted.

A quiet time on my own terms was just another place I could control. On my terms alone, it had become lifeless, stagnant, and boring. On my terms, it was a monologue instead of what it's meant to be—a dialogue between my Heavenly Papa and me.

On God's terms, spending time with Him is meant to be a living, fluid relationship filled with intimate conversations.

Nonetheless, I was hesitant to change. What if His overwhelming love interrupted my religious routine? By going through the motions of my quiet time rituals, I had created for myself a false sense of stability, security, and even righteousness.

Havilah Cunnington cautions, "Don't let the method [of your quiet times] become more important than the Message."

My methods had indeed become more important. I definitely had things out of order.

God is Not a Miser

Like the elder brother in the Parable of the Prodigal Son, we can even be living in God's house and still miss our Father's heart.

When the elder brother heard music and dancing in the prodigal's honor

> "[he] became angry and refused to go in. So his father went out and pleaded with him. But he answered his father, 'Look! All these years I've been slaving for you and never disobeyed your orders. Yet you never gave me even a young goat so I could celebrate with my friends'" (Luke 15:28-29).

After all his hard work and striving to do what is right in order to earn his father's love, he watches it freely and extravagantly given to a brother whose actions don't deserve it. The elder brother feels entitled to the father's blessings based on all his years of work. He isn't relying on grace but instead is working for position and privilege.

He isn't relying on grace but instead is working for position and privilege.

His worldview is challenged and he's angry. The elder brother has been so wrapped up in his own performance that he's missed the love of his father available to him all along.

Rather than focusing on his connection with the father as a son, he emphasizes his labor and obedience to justify his worth and value in the household. His performance had replaced authentic relationship with his dad. He views his role as son as one that has to be earned rather than simply received.

> "'My son,' the father said, 'You are always with me, and everything I have is yours'" (Luke 15:31).

When we're focused on performance, we keep track of our own rights and wrongs. When we do, we are bound to the law of sowing and reaping.[3] However, God's love "keeps no record of wrongs."[4] In fact, there's a higher law that supersedes the law of sowing and reaping. It's called grace. We encounter this grace at the cross of Jesus.

Kris Vallotton says, "When we enter into reaping what we didn't sow that's when we enter into inheritance." When we demand God only gives us what our good works deserve, we miss out on stepping into what we don't deserve, the fullness of our inheritance given to us by the hand of grace.

Jesus spoke to Paul on the road to Damascus while he was

3. Galatians 6:7
4. 1 Corinthians 13:5

persecuting Christians and told him the purpose behind his conversion was,

> "'to open their eyes so that they may turn from darkness to light and from the dominion of Satan to God, that they may receive forgiveness of sins and an inheritance among those who have been sanctified by faith in Me'" (Acts 26:18, NASB).

We access our inheritance by faith and grace. He forgives our sins in order to bring us into our spiritual inheritance. He saves us from sin in order to bring us into eternal life—not just in heaven but in the here and now. We don't get what our sins deserve.[5]

He rescues us from death and Satan's dark dominion in order to bring us into the arms of our Father. Here, we get abundant life in the Father's house as daughters.

> "I have come that they may have life and have it abundantly" (John 10:10, NASB).

The Fullness of the Father's Heart

Reliance on performance is kin to fear of lack. Fear of lack lies to us. It tells us there's not enough—not enough encounters, not enough revelation, not enough privilege, not enough love to go around.

The elder brother is too willing to settle for "not enough"—a goat rather than the fullness of the heart of his father who would have given him, like his prodigal brother, the fattened calf.

> "For it is by grace you have been saved, through faith—and this is not from yourselves, it is the gift of God— not by works, so that no one can boast" (Ephesians 2:8-9).

5. Romans 6:23

The good father in the parable extended grace to the prodigal who knew he wasn't worthy but humbly received it anyway. Whereas the grace that had always been available to the elder brother had been overlooked. He never tapped into all the father had wanted to give him because performance had twisted his perspective of himself and his father's heart.

God is not a miser who withholds but a good father who gives generously to everyone who asks Him

Like the elder brother in the parable, my own reliance on my quiet time performance along with my view of God as a closefisted father kept me from experiencing the feast in His Word. God is not a miser who withholds but a good father who gives generously to everyone who asks Him.[6]

He wants our time spent with Him to be rich and abundant. He wants us to relate to Him as a daughter to her father. That's His heart for us.

We need to allow ourselves to be adopted. We have to stop living like daughters of the father of lies.[7] It's time to come home to Love, God, our true Father, now and forever more.[8]

"No one can work their way into (God's) family, we must be born into it."[9] To be born again actually means to be reborn into God's very own family.[10]

When the Plan Backfires

One way God reveals His nature during childhood is through a child's parents. Family is meant to be a place of encounter

---

6. James 1:5
7. John 8:44
8. Isaiah 9:6
9. Lucille Travis, *George Whitefield: The Voice that Woke the World*, 2001.
10. John 3:3

with God through the consistent, loving care of our mother and father. In fact, Focus on the Family affirms, "parents are the single most important developmental influence in a child's life, apart from the Holy Spirit himself."[11]

As a child, it was only natural for me to project how I related to my parents onto how I related to God. This progression of learning and its application is how He designed things. But sometimes this plan backfires. Instead of finding the true God, we encounter a distorted image of Him that we internalize as truth. We grow up believing lies about God and His ways due to the sinfulness of man.

There are no perfect parents. I know that for a fact now that I've become a parent. We are all created in His image, but due to sinful choices, we don't always display His likeness.

The good news is God can use even a broken childhood to demonstrate His nature.

> "But he said to me, 'My grace is sufficient for you, for my power is made perfect in weakness'" (2 Corinthians 12:9).

The contrast of His light and truth against any darkness in our childhood experiences is beautifully distinct. However, it may seem muddled and gray in our present, everyday life. That's why we just need Holy Spirit to help us separate the truth from the lies.

Thankfully, He will always redeem and restore what was lost. He will spend a lifetime introducing you to His true nature. It is His plan and His delight. Jesus told the Father,

> "I have made your very being known to them—who you are and what you do—and continue to make it known, so that your love for me might be in them exactly as I am in them" (John 17:26, MSG).

11. Focusonthefamily.com/parenting/teens/your-teen-needs-you/build-your-teens-identity

God Calls You Daughter

A servant just does what her master tells her. It's a relationship based on obedience and fear of punishment. On the contrary, a friend is welcome to sit at the table and share in a conversation.

> "I have never called you 'servants,' because a master doesn't confide in his servants, and servants don't always understand what the master is doing. But I call you my most intimate friends, for I reveal to you everything that I've heard from my Father" (John 15:15, TPT).

The footnote in the Passion Translation for the above verse explains the origin and deeper meaning of "intimate friends" about whom Jesus spoke: "Both the Aramaic and Greek word for 'intimate friends' is actually 'those cared for from the womb.' You are more than a friend to him, for you were born again from his wounded side."[12]

Daughters have intimate access to the Master who now can call Him Papa

Because of Jesus's death and resurrection, we move from servant to friend—a friend who knows what the Master is doing. That in itself requires a rebirth because before we were friends of God, each of us was an enemy.

> "For if, while we were God's enemies, we were reconciled to him through the death of his Son, how much more, having been reconciled, shall we be saved through his life!" (Romans 5:10).

His death brought us new life and a new status before Him. Better yet, He even calls us His daughters. Daughters have

---

12. Brian Simmons, *John: Eternal Love* (The Passion Translation).

connection point
Salvation

Perhaps you're reading this book desiring relationship with God and yet realize that you've never actually responded to God's invitation for salvation. Or, you've responded but have been living away from God. Today's your day to come home!

He loves you and wants you to be a part of His forever family. He loves you so much He came to rescue you from being a slave to sin so He could make you His daughter living at home in His house.

On your own, you can't be good enough to enter the Kingdom of God. Salvation is a gift, not by works.[1]

He died so that you might live.[2] Not just eek by but really live, abundantly and victoriously.[3] He rose again so you'd have the power to do so.

A Prayer to Receive Salvation

Pray: "Jesus, thank You for dying for my sins. Forgive my sins and wash me with Your blood so I am as white as snow.[4] I want a new start, a new life with You. A new heart that completely belongs to You. Fill me with Your Holy Spirit, Your resurrection power and life![5] I'm in Your family now. You are my true Father and I am Your daughter. Thank You for making a way for me to live in intimate relationship with You.[6] I'm ready to start knowing You deeply today."

1. Ephesians 2:8-9
2. John 3:16
3. John 10:10
4. Isaiah 1:18
5. John 20:22
6. John 14:6

intimate access to the Master who now can call Him Papa.

> "The Spirit you received does not make you slaves, so that you live in fear again; rather, the Spirit you received brought about your adoption to sonship. And by him we cry, 'Abba, Father'" (Romans 8:15).

To move from servant to friend to a daughter filled with His Spirit, I had to be willing to let go of the reins and trust Him.

"His left hand cradles my head while his right hand holds me close. I am at rest in this love" (Song of Songs 2:6, TPT).

In the embrace of Love, the fear of punishment for not measuring up fades and we become unconditionally accepted and enjoyed. His embrace is the place we were created for.

Striving ceases in the arms of Love

"If we are afraid, it is for fear of punishment, and this shows that we have not fully experienced his perfect love" (1 John 4:18, NLT).

When we live in fear's embrace, we cannot be deeply aware of His arms of love. Fear gets in the way.

Striving ceases in the arms of Love. Instead of striving, I get to rest, sink into, let down in God's love that cradles me so tenderly and holds me so close. Here, in this Love, my guard comes down. God's embrace is complete. He holds all of me—even the parts where I've experienced shame because His "perfect love casts out our fear."[13]

Performance will lose its grip on you because you'll become more aware of God's passionate hold of you instead

When trust has been broken, it's difficult to rest. Instead, you're consumed with self-protection. You're afraid someone will hurt you, manipulate and control you, or make you feel responsible for what isn't yours.

Dodging dangers, whether they're physical, spiritual, or emotional, takes so much energy. No wonder fear keeps us on the move. Rest can only be found when we're enveloped in Love.

13. 1 John 4:18, ESV

As you encounter God's deep, unceasing, unchanging love for you, performance will fade. It will lose its grip on you because you'll become more aware of God's passionate hold of you instead. After all, performance has been only a poor substitute for an authentic relationship with Father God. A piddly attempt to earn His love. The more I trust and rest in His perfect and complete love of me the less I am driven to work for love. It's already mine, based not on what I do, but what He's done. My freedom from performance has been this type of journey. We don't need to battle performance to break free. We just need to come Home.

Living the Christian life without Holy Spirit's empowerment leads us back into performance

Depending on where we are in our healing, our homecoming may take time. Needless to say, the amount of time it takes is insignificant. What's important is simply our "yes" to God's embrace of relationship with us. We need to stop earning it, running from it, or trying to survive without it.

We need to come, fall desperately into His arms, and hold tight to His grip on us. We may need to do that over and over again until we are at home in those arms. It's the vantage point from which we were made to do life and to rule and reign with Him—in His big, strong Daddy arms.[14]

Overcoming Performance

Living the Christian life without Holy Spirit's empowerment leads us back into performance. We need Holy Spirit to take us from fear into family.

14. Ephesians 2:6

connection point
Baptism of the Holy Spirit

The Christian life is impossible to live without Holy Spirit's power. On our own, our best efforts only lead us back to striving and performance. We revert back to being law keepers rather than children of the King motivated to obedience by love.

> Jesus told us, "whoever believes in me will do the works I have been doing, and they will do even greater things than these" (John 14:12).

In our own abilities, we cannot live as Jesus lived. In our own strength, we cannot perform His miracles and even greater miracles.[1] Imagine that! Even greater things! Wow!

> "And with that [Jesus] breathed on [the disciples] and said, 'Receive the Holy Spirit'" (John 20:22).

Everyone receives the Holy Spirit when she believes. This is what it means to be born again. The fruit of the Spirit is evidence of Holy Spirit in your life.[2] Every believer should be bearing lots of good fruit!

After Jesus's resurrection, He reappeared to the disciples and reassured them,

> "But you will receive power when the Holy Spirit comes on you" (Acts 1:8).

The baptism of the Holy Spirit is power. With it comes numerous gifts! It's a dunking, immersing, and soaking in His presence. Like a sponge, we absorb Him. He fills our spirit with His.

It's a super-charged impartation of God's Spirit which gives us gifts to use in the church and the world and empowers us to live as Jesus lived.

> "I [John the Baptist] baptize you with water, but he [Jesus] will baptize you with the Holy Spirit" (Mark 1:8).

We need His power to live the victorious Christian life.

Baptism of the Holy Spirit in Action

Step 1: Receive the Holy Spirit.

Pray, "Thank You Jesus for coming and rising from the dead so I could be baptized with the Holy Spirit. I want Your presence and power in my life. I

---

1. John 14:12
2. Galatians 5:22-23

receive a fresh filling of Your Holy Spirit right now. I am excited to receive all the gifts You have for me."

Step 2: Receive Holy Spirit's gifts.

Read 1 Corinthians 12:7-11. Ask yourself, "Which gift(s) would I especially like to receive?" I want to encourage you to choose at least one.

Step 3: Hold out your hands like you're receiving a gift.

Pray: "Holy Spirit, I'd like to receive ____(name the gift). Teach me how to use it. With You, I want to discover everything about this gift. Thank you for this present. I receive it by faith."

Trust Holy Spirit to be your teacher.[3] The unwrapping of the gift involves a journey. It's an unpacking of the treasures He put inside of you when you received it. Holy Spirit is the instruction manual. It's amazing to experience how eager He is to give the gifts and grow them in our life.

He'll lead you to people who are more mature in the gift you've received to model it and teach you. He'll direct you to Scripture, books, and testimonies about the gift. He'll prompt you to pull it out and put it to use in a conversation or church setting.

As you trust Him and respond in obedience to His promptings, He'll instruct you as you go and weave it into the fabric of your life. Soon, you won't be able to fathom life without the continual infilling of Holy Spirit and His gifts.

> "And don't think he rations out the Spirit in bits and pieces. The Father loves the Son extravagantly. He turned everything over to him so he could give it away—a lavish distribution of gifts. That is why whoever accepts and trusts the Son gets in on everything, life complete and forever!" (John 3:34-36, MSG).

3. John 14:26

> "The Spirit himself testifies with our spirit that we are God's children" (Romans 8:16).

To testify means to declare, profess, or acknowledge openly.[15] One of Holy Spirit's jobs is to declare to our spirit who we are. This is another reason why the declarations we make over ourselves are so powerful. They can speak right into our spirits. The Bible tells us Holy Spirit is speaking into us our true identity as His daughter.

15. Testify. Dictionary.com

He has lovingly been speaking this over you since the moment you were born again, "You are mine. You are loved. You belong to me. You're my daughter."

Can you hear Him? At the beginning of my journey out of performance into living as a daughter, I approached being a daughter as something I still needed to achieve. Would I ever learn?

I determined, "I'll try really hard to learn to be a daughter." And then I had one. Camille Rose was born after a long line of six sons. She's been a gift to me for so many reasons. The gift most dear to my heart is that she teaches me how to be a daughter.

Not once have I seen Camille face the day working hard at being a daughter. She doesn't have to try. She simply is one and she never doubts it. It's not a mental undertaking but something she knows deep down.

Perhaps it's because we delight in speaking over her who she is.

"You're my girl!" I say as I squeeze her and hold her close. "You have a special place in our family," I remind her as her brothers go marching off to work on the farm without her because she's not old enough yet to catch chickens herself. Her older brother, Caleb, will spontaneously shout, "I love you little Miller" (her nickname) and smother her with kisses.

Because we've been loving her and speaking life over her even before she was born, she's secure in our love. She receives it without question and willingly comes back for more.

We learn who we are in His presence

Camille's life has been a glimpse to me of what being a daughter looks like. We can live like that too. The results of listening to Holy Spirit's words is deep security as daughters in the family of our Father. If we listen long enough, we'll start believing it. Our belief in God's truth will open our eyes to His love. A love perhaps we haven't been able to see or experience before because of lies we've been believing instead.

We learn who we are in His presence. Our own identity stems from who He is:

> "The Father, from whom every family in heaven and on earth derives its name" (Ephesians 3:14-15).

A strong sense of family identity is the outcome of a good relationship with one's father. Therefore, knowing our Father intimately also assists us in finding our place in His family—the church. We'll feel like we belong, sense our unique contribution, and love our sisters and brothers better as we believe Papa deeply loves us and divinely places us here.

Self-Discovery Questions

Before you begin, pray: "Papa God, give me eyes that see and ears that hear what You're saying to my spirit.[1] I also ask You for faith to believe it along with courage to renounce any lies I've been believing about You or myself."

1. Have my quiet time methods become more important than the Message? If so, how?
2. Do I find myself most often working from God's love or for it? What does it feel like?
3. In drawing close to Jesus, is there anything I am afraid of? (rejection, exposure of my true self, intimacy, etc.)
4. What past experiences in my childhood or otherwise may have caused me to adopt a performance mind-set?

1. Isaiah 6:9-10

5. As a result, is there anyone I need to forgive for teaching me this mind-set or modeling it for me to imitate? (See Connection Point: Forgiveness p. 47.)

   Pray: "Jesus, I forgive _____(name the person) for_____ (name the offense). I release him/her to You and I ask You to bless him/her."

6. Do I feel God withholds Himself from me in any way as I come to spend time with Him? As a result, have I settled for less or am I harboring offense towards Him? Describe. (Ask His forgiveness if you need to using Connection Point: Repentance p. 44.)

7. Right now, how do I view myself? As God's servant, as God's friend, or as God's daughter? Why am I most comfortable relating to God in this way?

Ask Holy Spirit Questions

Make a chart. Draw two columns and label one "Lie" and the other "Truth." Under the heading "Lie," list any lies Holy Spirit reveals as you ask Him the first two questions.

1. What lies am I believing about You and Your love for me?

2. What lies am I believing about my worth and value to You?

   Through the blood of Jesus and by the power of His name, break agreement with these lies that have held you bound in performance. (See Connection Point: Exchanging Lies for Truth p. 71.)

   Pray: "In the name of Jesus, I renounce the lie that You are/I am _____(name the lie). I break any partnership I've formed with this lie through my thoughts, attitudes, words, or actions, known or unknown. I break the power of the lie and cancel its assignment against me."

Take each individual lie you listed and ask God, "What is the truth about You (or me) instead?"

Under the heading "Truth," list the truths that trump each lie in your life. Write any Scriptures echoing or reinforcing them.

Because Holy Spirit is testifying to your spirit, also ask Him, "Holy Spirit, what are You speaking over me?"[2] This question is another way of uncovering His truth. List His responses on your chart.

3.   What do you want me to know and experience about the Father's love for me? For starters, picture yourself in Love's arms. What does it look like? What does it feel like to be held by God? Who's holding you (Father God, Jesus, or Holy Spirit)? Draw it or describe your experience.

Pray

"Thank You God for making me Your daughter. I want to hear what You're speaking deep into my spirit. I receive everything You have for me. I want to be at home in Your arms. Thank You that there is no longer anything that can separate me from Your love. Your truth sets me free!"[3]

Declarations

- My strivings cease when I rest in God's love for me.[4]

- The time I spend with God is rich and abundant. He speaks to me and I hear Him. We share an intimate dialogue that satisfies my soul.[5]

Step Into Freedom

2. John 8:16
3. John 8:32; Romans 8:16; Luke 15:31
4. Song of Songs 2:6; 1 John 4:18
5. Psalms 63:3-5; Psalms 84:10

Choose to do at least one this week.

MAKE POWERFUL DECLARATIONS OVER YOUR LIFE

Turn the truths Holy Spirit showed you into transformational declarations. Creatively write them on note cards, in the margins of your Bible, on signs around your home, or in your Quiet Time Journal.

Check out the ideas on my Pinterest board for making your declarations into works of art: pinterest.com/snmothering/quiet-time-book-crafts/

The important thing is to keep them before you. Repeat them as you go through your day, especially when you feel the lie trying to creep in again. Let the truth of God transform your mind and therefore begin to transform your life! To assist you, see Connection Point: Making Declarations p. 28.

KEEP GETTING TO THE ROOT

As we take this journey toward freedom, sometimes we realize the things holding us back are more than we can tackle on our own. I've been there. I want to encourage you to make a phone call to a friend or pastor for healing prayer.

Or, seek out your church's inner healing ministry or local Sozo ministry for additional help. Sozo originated at Bethel Church, Redding, CA (bethelsozo.com). It is a unique inner healing and deliverance ministry aimed at getting to the root of things hindering your personal connection with the Father, Son, and Holy Spirit.

As God brings pain to the surface, trust He has a purpose and wants to bring healing to you at this time. Partner with Him and ask for the help you need.

What will you do this week to bring you more healing?

Journal

What did you learn? In your Quiet Time Journal, write what God did in your heart this week.

connection point
Exchanging Lies for Truth

God wants to silence any lies we're believing with His truth.[1] Unbelief (not believing His truth) separates us from Him.[2] Our beliefs drive our actions. Because what we believe, we become, we must guard our thought life.[3]

We must be vigilant about living out of truth rather than lies so our life reflects His Spirit. Lies bear destruction. Whereas truth brings forth life![4] When necessary, we can make this Connection Point a daily practice for maintaining our closeness to God.

> "Jesus answered, 'I am the way and the truth and the life. No one comes to the Father except through me'" (John 14:6).

Exchanging Lies for Truth in Action

Step 1: Discern the lie you're believing.

Describe any emotions, situations, memories, or patterns to help you.

For example, let's say you feel alone in your problems. Whenever you face a dilemma, you mildly panic, scrambling for solutions. So, you realize you're believing the lie that "God isn't enough for me when life is difficult."

Sometimes when our life has been entrenched in a lie for so long, it can be tough discerning the truth. To help you find the truth, try boiling the lie down to one sentence or even one word.

For example, using the above, you might conclude the lie is "God is insufficient" or "God doesn't care."

Step 2: Repent of believing the lie.

The purpose of repenting is to turn away from the lie so you can turn towards truth instead.

Pray: "God, please forgive me for believing (name the lie). In the name

1. Psalms 63:11
2. Hebrews 3:7-19
3. Proverbs 23:7
4. John 10:10

of Jesus, I break any partnership I've formed with this lie through my thoughts, attitudes, words, or actions, known or unknown. I break the power of the lie and cancel its assignment against me."

Step 3: Recognize the truth.

To do so, frequently, the truth is the opposite of the lie.

For example, if the lie is "God is insufficient," then the truth is "God is sufficient. He is enough." Or if the lie is "God doesn't care," then the truth is "God does care. He intimately knows me and cares for me."

Step 4: Find a verse in the Bible or a name of God representing His character to support and validate the truth.

For example, God reveals Himself as El-Shaddai to Abraham in Genesis 17:1,

> "When Abram was ninety-nine years old, the Lord appeared to him and said, "I am God Almighty [In Hebrew: El-Shaddai]; walk before me faithfully and be blameless."

Seek more understanding through your study. For example, a note from a study Bible tells us, "Another word much like Shaddai, and from which many believe it derived, is shad meaning "breast" in Hebrew. This refers to God completely nourishing, satisfying, and supplying His people with all their needs as a mother would her child. Connected with the word for God, El, this denotes a God who freely gives nourishment and blessing, He is our sustainer." [5]

Or, for the lie, "God doesn't care," you could use the verse,

> "Give all your worries and cares to God, for he cares about you" (1 Peter 5:7, NLT).

You can turn this truth into a declaration: "When life is difficult, God is my El-Shaddai. He sustains me and nourishes me with more than enough."

Or "God cares about my problems. I give my worries to Him and He tenderly takes care of my needs."

For more tips for turning truth into declarations, see Connection Point: Making Declarations p. 28.

Step 5: Sustain the truth of God in your life.

As soon as you find yourself living out of the lie again, repent using the prayer in step two.

Take up the truth instead. Remind your spirit of who God says He is or who He says you are. Don't worry if you find yourself needing to do this several times. You're doing battle with some enemies in your promised land. They will topple with the truth, but they may not fall without a fight.

5. Blueletterbible.org/study/misc/name_god.cfm

four

Misunderstanding God's Heart

No one likes to be misunderstood. How many marriage conflicts could I have avoided had I taken time to really listen and understand my husband's perspective rather than assume I somehow knew what was in his heart? In marriage, a misunderstanding can easily lead to disconnection if we don't proactively seek to value each other's viewpoint.

Likewise, we can develop obstacles to deeper connection with God when we misunderstand His heart. In our journey after God, we must, first and foremost, be seekers of His heart. However, if we filter God's Word or His responses to our prayers through past hurts and disappointments, our perception of God's heart can become distorted.

As a result, we may misunderstand who He truly is. Any misunderstanding of who He is also limits our experience of everything He has for us. We see this from the very beginning. It was Satan's strategy from day one.

> "And the Lord God commanded the man, 'You are free
> to eat from any tree in the garden; but you must not

eat from the tree of the knowledge of good and evil, for when you eat from it you will certainly die" (Genesis 2:16-17).

Adam and Eve traded the truth of God as a loving creator for the lie that God's heart wasn't for them. They also exchanged the truth of His complete abundance for them (since they were free to eat from any tree in the garden except one) for the lie that God was keeping something good from them. The serpent caused them to doubt God's heart and His perfect design by asking, "Did God really say...?" and twisting the truth into a crafty lie.[1]

Any misunderstanding of who He is also limits our experience of everything He has for us

Satan uses this same strategy with us. We can find ourselves being mistrustful of God's heart and questioning God's design of our own identity. Consequently, the truth of who God is and of who we are becomes distorted and we can find ourselves living out of a lie. The lie then disconnects us from His heart.

After they ate from the tree, Adam and Eve's own sin and their misunderstanding of God's heart toward them caused them to run and hide when they heard God coming.

> "Then the man and his wife heard the sound of the Lord God as he was walking in the garden in the cool of the day, and they hid from the Lord God among the trees of the garden. But the Lord God called to the man, 'Where are you?'...The Lord God made garments of skin for Adam and his wife and clothed them...After he drove the man out, he placed on the east side of the Garden of Eden

1. Genesis 3:1-5

cherubim and a flaming sword flashing back and forth to guard the way to the tree of life" (Genesis 3:8-9, 21, 24).

God not only initiates relationship with us but pursues and restores it when it's in jeopardy. When Adam and Eve's disobedience and unbelief separated them from Him, God made the first animal sacrifice to cleanse and clothe them. He guarded the Tree of Life from them so they wouldn't eat of its fruit and live forever in a state of disconnection from His presence.

The rest of the Bible is a love story of God's continual initiation, His romantic pursuit, and our complete reconciliation to Him. Why would we think our own story would be any different?

Food from Heaven

God is passionate about bringing His truth to places in our hearts where we've believed lies. The most destructive lies we internalize are those about God and about our own identity. Our beliefs about who God is and who we are ultimately dictate how we choose to live and how we fulfill our destinies.

Recently, I went away to a women's retreat. While there, I attended a session about encountering God in His Word. I was hungry to meet God in the Bible. My quiet times had been up and down. Sometimes God's Word and His presence felt so alive that I couldn't wait to get away with Him. Other times, the Bible felt two-dimensional. Reading it felt more like a discipline than a way to encounter a tangible relationship with Jesus.

The speaker encouraged us to ask God what He wanted us to read. Then, we were to go and read it, if possible, in one sitting, digesting a full meal of Scripture.

I asked God and He highlighted Song of Songs to me. The day before the main speaker had mentioned a study about Song of Songs and I had made a note of it. It was a book that has always intrigued me but I didn't fully grasp its content. I felt it contained many secrets to be unlocked and to be honest, I was a little intimidated by it. When I asked God what to read, almost instantly this book that had tugged at my heart the day before popped into my mind. Trusting it was God's leading, I opened my Bible to Song of Songs chapter one.

I read four chapters but just couldn't imagine reading all eight in one sitting. (I don't usually read more than a chapter of the Bible at a time so this was already a stretch for me.) In fact, I didn't end up reading it all at once but finished it over the course of a few days.

I was wondering why I didn't have the vigor and the passion to devour it all at once as the session's speaker had described to be her own experience. What was holding me back from all eight chapters when it was as if God Himself was inviting me into His mysteries and promising to help decode them? Why would I linger around the perimeter, just getting my toes wet when He was inviting me to take the plunge into His Word?

As I pondered these questions, I recognized previously, when I did experience God's presence in His Word and heard His voice, I would stop short. I wouldn't finish the meal. I would take small bites of Scripture because I wanted to stretch out the goodness. This may seem noble and super spiritual. In reality, deep down, my reason for responding to Scripture reading this way was rooted in fear. I was afraid the feast wouldn't equally be available to me the next time I came.

I wasn't sure why God sometimes felt more present in the Scriptures than at other times. If He met me in one passage, I'd fear I might not find Him again in another. He felt so unpredictable.

His freedom to choose how and where He met me challenged my attempts to find security in being in control and in charge. I had been seeking control in other areas of my life as well.

Naturally, my need for control tried to play itself out in my most intimate human relationship—my marriage. I love to hear my husband share his heart with me. Sometimes, because his response may not

The environment created by control might be nice and tidy but relationships become barren under the spirit of control and manipulation

be exactly what I'm wanting to hear, I'll disagree and wrongly try to manipulate his point of view. I feel perfectly justified in my reasoning until he remarks, "You can't take away my freedom to express my opinion."

In those moments, I realize I'm trying to control his responses to me. Control creates a sterile environment. The environment created by control might be nice and tidy but relationships become barren under the spirit of control and manipulation. I didn't want that in my marriage. I certainly didn't want it in my relationship with God. I want to give God the freedom to be God, not a version of one I can control.

Out of fear, manipulation, and control, I tried to ration out my encounter with God in His Word. Still, I can't put God in a Ziploc bag to save for later.

> "You alone are the Lord. You made the heavens, even the highest heavens, and all their starry host, the earth and all that is on it, the seas and all that is in them. You give life to everything, and the multitudes of heaven worship you" (Nehemiah 9:6).

Through my approach to Scripture reading, though it was a "spiritual endeavor," I was trying to control the God who made the heavens and the earth, our limitless God who just won't fit in a bag or a box.

So, when I return the next morning for my quiet time leftovers and go back to the same passage that had been so alive the day before, the encounter can feel stale, like it's past its prime and I've missed something. That was my actual experience.

Nevertheless, my experience wasn't a true reflection of His nature. Because He wasn't going to be bound to a quiet time on my terms, I believed Him to be inconsistent, indifferent, and uncaring. My belief in this lie about His character caused me to pull away from our connection. Clearly, I had misunderstood God's heart.

> "The Lord said to Moses, 'Look, I'm going to rain down food from heaven for you. Each day the people can go out and pick up as much food as they need for that day...' Then Moses added, 'The Lord will give you meat to eat in the evening and bread to satisfy you in the morning'" (Exodus 16: 4, 8, NLT).

Even though we can't control how or when God encounters us, there's always spiritual food available whenever we're hungry, whenever we need it. There's "bread" enough for today. So, eat and be satisfied. Trust there will be "bread" on the table of tomorrow as well. He will provide.

In his book *Translating God*, Shawn Bolz says, "God want[s] to converse with us about his heart—not just show it to us in the Scriptures, but bring the Scriptures alive through his Spirit!"[2]

---

2. Shawn Bolz, *Translating God: Hearing God's Voice for Yourself and the World Around You*, 2015.

He is good. He wants to show up. He wants to talk with us as we read the Bible and make the Scriptures come alive to us through His Spirit. He'll do it in His way and on His terms. His every action and response to us is with a heart full of undying love.

As we begin to grasp that and truly believe it, it's easier to let go of the reins and let God out of the bag we've put Him in. When we do, He'll surprise us in unexpected ways and take us on unimaginable adventures. So, let's lay down control and say yes to freedom!

Peanut Butter & Jelly Quiet Times

Because I've struggled to believe everything He has is mine, I've been too easily satisfied with less. If I didn't meet God in His Word, I wouldn't persevere but would almost give up. I'd close His Book having nourished my soul with truth and life-giving principles but missing my Lover.

It was like I had filled a hole in my stomach with nutrients that would sustain me but I didn't feel satisfied like I had enjoyed a juicy prime rib. It was my peanut butter and jelly quiet time. I wasn't necessarily hungry after that meal but I wasn't really satisfied either.

Instead of pursuing God for more of what I needed and desired, I settled for less.

> "One night as I lay in bed, I yearned for my lover. I yearned for him, but he did not come. So I said to myself, 'I will get up and roam the city, searching in all its streets and squares. I will search for the one I love. So I searched everywhere but did not find him. The watchmen stopped me as they made their rounds, and I asked, 'Have you seen the one I love?' Then scarcely had I left them when I found

my love! I caught and held him tightly, then I brought him to my mother's house, into my mother's bed, where I had been conceived" (Song of Songs 3:1-4, NLT).

This passage is a beautiful picture of our intimacy with God. When we long for God to show up and instead He feels distant, I believe He is actually wooing us closer to Himself and deeper into His heart. He wants us to pursue Him.

Previously, when God felt far off, I'd internalize it as His rejection of me or indifference toward me. Because of my frame of understanding created by the wounds from my past, I had misunderstood His heart. Pursuit requires trust. Although He could outsmart me, like a good Father He lets Himself be found. Instead, He is only whispering from afar, "Here I am. Come a little closer."

With a true understanding of His heart toward me, moments of unmet expectations can be instead received as invitations to search unceasingly for Him everywhere with the longing of a lover.

Notice what happens in the Song of Songs after the Beloved pursues her Lover. She holds on tight and brings him home to her mother's bed. This is a place where more is unveiled, more is revealed, and more is received. It is a picture of oneness.

Do you want more of God? Don't be afraid to pursue Him. Your quest will be rewarded with increased trust and greater intimacy.

> "And without faith it is impossible to please God, because anyone who comes to him must believe that he exists and that he rewards those who earnestly seek him" (Hebrews 11:6).

Hide & Seek

Relationship with Jesus sometimes involves a game of hide and seek. Not because He's cruel and leaves us out in the cold. It's because He has more for us and wants us to learn how to draw near—how to be like the young woman in the passage above in hot pursuit of her lover. He will reward you with more than you could ask or imagine as you seek Him.

Bill Johnson says, "God doesn't hide things from us. He hides things for us."[3]

Even in the Bible, it can seem as if Jesus is hiding only to reveal He has a greater purpose and plan. Lazarus is sick and Jesus tarries two days before going to help. By then, Lazarus had died. The Bible even tells us, "Jesus loved Mary, Martha, and Lazarus with a divine love" yet still He waited to come.[4]

The disciples with Jesus didn't understand.

When we don't understand why our quiet times don't go the way we want, we need to trust His heart

> "Then Jesus made it plain to them, 'Lazarus is dead. And for your sake, I'm glad I wasn't there, because now you have another opportunity to see who I am so that you will learn to trust in me" (John 11:14-15, TPT).

Jesus lingered not because he was too busy or unfeeling but because He wanted to reveal more of Himself to those He loved. When we don't understand why our quiet times don't go the way we want, we need to trust His heart.

To quote Bill Johnson again, "Mystery is as important as revelation. Because mystery is where your trust is proven."

Jesus feels compassion and tenderness over any sorrow or

3. Reference to Proverbs 25:2
4. John 11:5-6, TPT

disappointment we might experience. Yet, He may hold off because He has something deeper and even more spectacular to show us about Himself. The woman left her bed and roamed the damp, dark city in the dead of night looking for her lover. God may want our passion and longing for Him to grow so we are willing to sacrifice for love like she did.

When Jesus doesn't respond just the way Mary and Martha want Him to, they rationalize, "if you'd only been here..."[5] Yet, had He shown up on the scene a few days earlier, they would never have witnessed God's power and love manifested in Lazarus's resurrection.

Likewise, if we've misunderstood His heart, we may easily become offended and harden our own hearts when God doesn't respond the way we want. Ultimately, these moments of disappointment or dissatisfaction cause us to search our hearts. At those times, we become distinctly aware of our own need to settle the issue that we are indeed truly loved and He is completely good and trustworthy.

Faith views lack as an opportunity for Jesus to reveal who He is in the situation

If these fundamental beliefs are in question in any way, we will receive any "hiding" God does as rejection or indifference rather than as an invitation to know Him more. When there is lack, faith views it as an opportunity for Jesus to reveal who He is in the situation.

So, let's believe like with Lazarus's resurrection, God wants to show us who He truly is so that we learn to completely trust in Him. He is good and He knows where He's leading us. Embrace the thrill of the hunt. Keep up your courage and go after Him. After all, you are loved and you can trust Him.

5. John 11:21

God Likes to Surprise You

We had just found out we were pregnant with our eighth baby and were planning to tell the kids that night. Joseph (then age six), usually the first one up, wandered into the quiet kitchen. Eagerly, he told me about his vivid dream and how God had showed him he was going to have another brother. I just about fell back against the counter.

The fact that God spoke to Joseph through his dream didn't surprise me. Ever since he was a baby, we've declared over him that God would reveal mysteries to him in the night hours since Joseph, the dreamer from the Bible, was his namesake. What surprised me was the timing of God's revelation to Joseph and the announcement that I was pregnant with our seventh son.

My heart's desire was to give our only daughter a sister. As wonderful as Joseph's encounter was, I had to admit I was a little disappointed. However, in the months that followed, I began relishing the idea of another son. I began resting in God's design for our family and even rejoicing in it.

Finally, the day came when we had our twenty-week ultrasound. Just my husband and I sat full of excitement in the room. Without a doubt, the technician reported we were having a girl. A torrent of varied emotions rushed in. Instantly, I felt ecstatic because this had been my original hope and prayer. On the heels of my excitement followed dread. Oh how would Joseph handle the news?

I agonized over how I would tell him so I could protect him from confusion and disappointment. How was this going to affect his relationship with God? We had treated Joseph's dream as truth, building him up about hearing from the Lord. How was I going to explain this?

The truth was I couldn't. I truly believed God spoke to

Joseph in his dream, revealing my pregnancy. I didn't understand myself why the dream seemed to reveal a son, rather than a daughter.

After dinner, the kids piled on the couch, impatient to finally hear the day's news. Joyfully, we told them they were going to be blessed with another sister. Immediately, I looked at Joseph. I locked my eyes with his and anxiously asked how he was feeling about the news.

His expression was thoughtful and then slowly a smile spread across his face. He announced with a laugh, "I guess God just wanted to surprise me!"

I was shocked. So this is what child-like faith looks like, right before my very eyes. Because Joseph didn't harbor any offense against God from past disappointments or misunderstandings, he received the news with complete trust in God's character.

Joseph undoubtedly believed God's heart was good. So, he filtered the mystery and the revelation of God through this lens. For Joseph, it was that easy. He was building his worldview circumstance upon circumstance on the precept that God is good all the time, even when we don't understand. I'm convinced this truth and trust in God's heart is enough to carry him through the rest of his life.

> "Mark this: Unless you accept God's kingdom in the simplicity of a child, you'll never get in" (Mark 10:15, MSG).

Like me, you may have made God in your own image, someone small enough to control. Or, maybe you've feared there was a limitation to His blessings towards you and so you've settled for less. It may be you've misunderstood Him as a disapproving Father who withholds his goodness rather than as a Lover wooing you closer with surprises and gifts.

Whatever the misunderstanding, God wants to reveal to you the truth about His heart. As you answer the following questions, take time to really search your own heart. Let Holy Spirit show you any lies or unbelief so you can relate to God more fully from a place of child-like faith and truth.

Self-Discovery Questions

Before you begin, pray: "Search me, O God, and know my heart; Try me and know my anxious thoughts; And see if there be any hurtful way in me, And lead me in the everlasting way."[1]

Once again, make a chart. Draw two columns and label one "Lie" and the other "Truth." Under the heading "Lie," list any lies Holy Spirit reveals as you ask yourself the following questions.

1. Am I afraid my encounter with Jesus in His Word today might not be available to me tomorrow? If yes, why? What's the lie I'm believing?

2. Are there any aspects of God I'm trying to control? If yes, which ones? (where, when, or how God encounters me with His presence, His forgiveness, His responses to my prayers, etc). What's the lie I'm believing?

3. Am I hesitant to seek after God for fear He'll reject me or not be everything I need? If yes, what is the lie?

    Repent for believing each of these lies. (For additional help, see Connection Point: Exchanging Lies for Truth p. 71.)

---

1. Psalm 139:23-24

Pray: "God, please forgive me for believing You are _____(name the misunderstanding: stingy, uncaring, unloving, unfaithful, etc.).

"Please forgive me for responding to you from this place of misunderstanding and for living out of that lie. In the name of Jesus, I break any partnership I've formed with this lie through my thoughts, attitudes, words, or actions, known or unknown. I break the power of the lie and cancel its assignment against me.

"I repent and let go of my attempts to control You. I want You to be free to be fully God in our relationship. Please forgive me for settling for less than You want me to have and/or for being offended at what You're doing or not doing in my life. Instead, I choose to trust You and believe there is more and that You are good."

Ask Holy Spirit Questions

For each lie written on your chart, ask God, "What is the truth about You instead?" Record the truths about Him in the column marked "Truth" in your journal. Ask yourself question 1 about each truth on your list.

1. How will this new truth change what I do? To help bring about these changes in your life, you may choose to turn the truths on your chart into declarations. (See Connection Point: Making Declarations p. 28.)

2. In our relationship, where am I doubting Your love for me?

3. In our relationship, where am I not trusting You?

4. If you feel like God is distant, ask Him, "When You're hiding, it's often because You have more for me. What do You want to show me about Yourself?"

Sin does separate us from God and hinders our intimate connection with Him. Along with the above question, you may also feel the need to ask Him, "Is there any sin in my life hindering our relationship that I need to repent of? (See Connection Point: Repentance p. 44.)

5. God, if You could play any game with me right now, what game would it be? Why did You pick this game? What is special about it? What do you want to teach me through this game?[2]

As God answers this question, let Him initiate the game and then, if you're willing, play it with Him. See what He has for you in this sacred moment.

Pray

"My misunderstandings of You have sometimes caused me to pull away. Instead of bringing me closer to you, at times I have felt distant from Your presence. I want to experience Your tangible love and everything You have for me. Thank you for paying a high price for me to be Your very own daughter. I'm looking forward to seeing You through new eyes—the eyes of truth. Holy Spirit, reveal to me more about my Father. I love you God!"[3]

Declarations

- When I seek after God, I find Him. He rewards my pursuit of Him by giving me more of Himself.[4]

- There is no lack in Jesus. Everything He has is mine.[5]

---

2. Activity adapted from *Eyes that See, Ears that Hear* by Jennifer Toledo
3. 1 Corinthians 6:19-20; Psalm 139: 7-12; 1 Corinthians 2:9-12
4. Psalms 34:8; Hebrews 11:6
5. Luke 15:31; Psalms 34:10

Step Into Freedom

Choose to do at least one this week.

Read Morning & Evening

Sandwich your day with God's Word! Read the Bible when you get up and read it again right before bed. Let His Word be the meditation of your heart. He wants to satisfy you with good things—bread in the morning and meat in the evening.

Finish Your Meal

Ask God which passage in the Bible to read. Then, read it all in one sitting. Take it all in until you feel full with God's Word. Take big bites and chew. Swallow. Enjoy. It's rich, so savor every morsel!

Play Hide & Seek with God

When you feel dissatisfied with the time you've spent with Jesus, keep seeking Him. Don't settle for less than experiencing His presence. As you continue throughout your day, keep your heart turned towards Him by playing hide and seek.

Look for Him in unexpected places. Go back to His Word and ask Holy Spirit to reveal God's heart for you. With the determination of a child, don't stop "playing" until you find Him! Keep the connection intact. Record this experience in your journal.

Read Between the Lines

Find Jesus on the pages of your Bible. This may seem obvious but I spent years diligently reading God's Word but less frequently experiencing His presence.

> "The Bible is a light for you—to help you 'see' Me better" (From Psalm 119:105, *Jesus Calling Bible Storybook* by Sarah Young).

We read the Bible to help us know the person of Jesus better, not just to know about Him or the right ways to live. Read a passage of Scripture and journal what it reveals to you about God. Then, praise Him for who He is. Tell Him you want to know this part of His heart better.

Journal

What did you learn? In your Quiet Time Journal, write which misunderstanding of God's heart from this chapter you identified with the most? How are you deliberately choosing to live from a new place of truth instead?

five

What Do You Really Want?

In relationship, when there is a lack of connection, it's easy to try and fill the space with duty and become task-oriented.

> "Cease striving and know that I am God" (Psalm 46:10, NASB).

In the Hebrew grammar, this verse is written in such a way as to tell us that we cease striving in order to know who He is. Striving gets in the way. When I stopped striving, I began knowing.

The word "know" in this verse is the same Hebrew word used in Genesis 4:1,

> "And Adam knew Eve his wife; and she conceived, and bare Cain, and said, I have gotten a man from the Lord" (KJV).

It's an intimate knowing by experience. This is the way God wants to be known by us.

To strive means to exert much effort or energy. During my quiet times, I certainly had been hard at work exerting much effort towards being good enough to be loved. It felt too vulnerable for me to just come right out and expose to Him my deepest needs for His love. All that hard work had actually been a cover-up for acknowledging my true needs to God and to myself.

> "See what great love the Father has lavished on us, that we should be called children of God! And that is what we are!" (I John 3:1).

If we are God's children, I wasn't acting much like one. I was comfortable acting as His servant and was uneasy being His child. A child simply asks and receives. A child simply trusts.

> "Which of you, if your son asks for bread, will give him a stone? Or if he asks for a fish, will give him a snake? If you, then, though you are evil, know how to give good gifts to your children, how much more will your Father in heaven give good gifts to those who ask him!" (Matthew 7:9-11).

It was time to start trusting, to start asking, to start receiving. He was my good Father with good gifts. After all, Psalms 103:5 proclaims God is the one "who satisfies your desires with good things." I didn't have to be afraid anymore.

When there is a lack of connection, it's easy to try and fill the space with duty and become task-oriented

However, I did have to stop striving. I had to stop focusing on doing and to start focusing on receiving so I could truly know Him.

Intimate connection with Jesus is our starting point, not our end reward. We don't have to earn it. It was given to us through the cross. I already had it. I only needed to believe and let my life-giving relationship with God grow in this soil.

Getting to the Heart of the Matter

In John chapter 1, two disciples of John the Baptist start following behind Jesus when John announces Jesus is the Lamb of God.

Jesus turned around and saw they were following Him and asked, "What do you want?" In the Message translation, it says He asked, "What are you after?"

Intimate connection with Jesus is our starting point, not our end reward

Now we all know Jesus knew why they were there. It seems silly He, the omniscient one, would even bother to ask that question. I believe He asked it not because He didn't know, but because He wanted them to know what was in their own hearts.

His purpose was to help them get in touch with their own desires and uncover their true spiritual hunger.

As you'll observe, the two disciples don't do a very good job answering. In fact, it appears they change the subject. They respond, "Rabbi, where are you staying?"

Maybe they didn't really know their answer to Jesus's question. Or maybe, they wanted to spend more time with Jesus yet didn't know how to exactly articulate their desires. Perhaps it was too just vulnerable to share why they had come. Whatever their reasons, clearly they were going to keep this conversation on the surface.

I love Jesus's response to their superficial question, "Come and discover for yourselves."

It's His open invitation for more. There's no wrong answer to His question, "What do you want?" Jesus doesn't lose patience with us as we're groping in the dark of our own desires. He just woos us in closer to His light.

If God is the great initiator, then we must learn to be great receivers and respond like children to His invitations. It's like He's saying to you and to me, "Come closer and discover everything you need and want here with me. I want you with me. It's okay if you don't know exactly why you've come. We'll spend a lifetime and eternity discovering together all that I am and have to offer you. Just come today. Let me steer the journey. You're made for this. It will be fun."[1]

God's invitation always initiates relationship

The two who ended up going with Him "saw where He was staying and spent the day with Him."[2]

God's invitation always initiates relationship, not just a momentary interaction but an entire day spent in His presence. These days add up to a lifetime.

Start the Dialogue with Jesus

Jesus has initiated relationship and you've responded. He's already started the conversation with you as well. So, let Him ask you, "What do you want?"

What is it that you want out of your quiet time with Him today? Why have you come? These are challenging questions to ask ourselves because they expose what's in our hearts.

The morning I read the above passage, I got teary and my voice cracked as I responded to Him, "I don't know. Why have I come?"

I thought a moment. Next month's income was questionable. We had recently moved to a new town. I had hung up a "Home Sweet Home" sign in our dining room in hopes that this town would truly become our long-term home.

"I need security," I answered.

---

1. John 17:24
2. John 1:39

For someone like me, having spent my childhood stuffing my own needs and desires while worrying about meeting the needs of others around me, it has been revolutionary to be able to know my own heart well enough to even answer this question.

Yes, we are prayer warriors, scholars of God's Word, intercessors, teachers, and much more. But that's not why we come.

First and foremost, we are daughters.

We come to experience the love of our Father. We come to get our core desires fulfilled, our deepest needs met in the arms of our Papa God. In Tony Stoltzfus's book *Questions for Jesus: Conversational Prayer Around Your Deepest Desires*, the author lists seventeen core desires we all experience:

- Worth
- Be Known
- Joy
- Love
- Comfort
- Belonging
- Peace
- Security
- To Come Through
- Goodness
- Recognition
- Approval
- Justice
- Freedom
- Significance
- Challenge
- Physical Needs

As mothers who diligently meet the numerous needs of others around us, this list validates our own deep desires too. There is no shame in having them. We were created with these needs. They are a fundamental part of who we are.

It's important to recognize them as driving forces in our everyday situations because often we look to other people or things to give us what God intended only Himself to perfectly fulfill. Ultimately, when we do this, it only leads

connection point
Identifying Your Core Desires

Identifying and validating our core desires is another key part of tending the garden of our heart and taking care of ourselves. When we are aware of what is going on inside of us, we can then choose to express our needs in a healthy way so those needs can be truly met.

If we aren't in tune with what we need or haven't established the practice of bringing it to Jesus, it's likely we'll resort to dishonest practices like manipulation and control to satisfy our core desire. Even when we aren't conscious of the need, it can still drive our actions.

Identifying Your Core Desires in Action

Step 1: Determine what you need.

For example, your day's schedule is full and you feel you need to simplify things.

Step 2: Ask yourself: "What will that give me?"[1]

Boil the desire down until you get to one or more of the "core desires" listed on p. 95. This is the heart of the issue. This is what you're really after. This is what only Jesus can truly satisfy in you through your relationship with Him.

For example, let's say you answer, "Simplifying will give me a more achievable list of obligations." Then ask yourself again, "What will that give me?" You answer, "It will give me a sense of accomplishment." And again, "What will that give me?" You answer, "A feeling of worth."

Step 3: Bring your core desire to Jesus.

Pray: "How do you want to meet my desire for ___(name the core desire) today?"

For example, He may respond with a reminder that your worth is not in what you accomplish but in who and Whose you are. Or you may feel the warmth of His love flooding your heart. Or you may feel Him holding the place that aches in His hands, not fixing it but just guarding it for what He has in store for you next.

If you had any trouble with this exercise, don't worry. There have been times when I didn't know what I needed even after I asked myself the question. In those cases, I've simply learned to ask Holy Spirit, "What do I need?" because He knows before I even ask Him and then listen. Even if you don't receive His immediate answer to this question, don't give up! Trust Him to reveal your own heart to you and to meet your needs. Sometimes, I don't hear an answer. Nonetheless, I will still experience His response and fulfillment of a need I couldn't even identify. The point is to expectantly bring your deep needs to Jesus and just let Him to do the rest.

---

1. Tony Stoltzfus, *Questions for Jesus: Conversational Prayer Around Your Deepest Desires*, 2013.

to disappointment and disillusionment. True, we may find temporary satisfaction but it won't last. It never does. We'll be left wanting, floundering for more. Jesus doesn't want to see us go through that. He made us for Himself. I've had to learn the hard way, but perhaps we all do. We learn that "because God made us for Himself, our hearts are restless until we rest in Him."[3]

God Holds the Answers You Need

When I brought Him my need for security that day and then asked Him how He wanted to meet my need, He reminded me of an encounter I had experienced with Him a few days prior.

The sky was gray and thick with clouds. I knew it was going to rain. We had been in a drought so the rain was needed and welcomed.

My husband is a farmer and had just introduced our new flock of chicks to pasture. They were a bit fragile and too ignorant to take shelter in a storm and we were worried how they would fare.

My neighbor sent me a text message and a picture of my house with a huge rainbow over it and said, "Look outside!" I ran outside and called the kids.

The rainbow was vibrant with color and looked as if it literally stretched end to end over our house. I took numerous photos and sent one to my husband saying, "God has covered us with His promises. His banner over us is love."

He was five miles down the road at the farm where he worked with our chickens. When he saw the rainbow, he told me he immediately thought the same thing about God's promises. My husband's response confirmed to me that God

---

3. Paraphrase of St. Augustine of Hippo, *Confessions:* "Thou hast made us for thyself, O Lord, and our heart is restless until it finds its rest in thee."

was indeed speaking to me through nature.

Soon, it started to drizzle and then came a short downpour. The rainbow faded. Normally, rainbows follow the rain. But I noticed how this rainbow had preceded the storm.

In my quiet time moment, he brought back the image of my home under His rainbow as a picture of security. I felt like God said the rain will come. However, His promises have preceded any storms we'll face. They are truer than the storms. I'm held safe and secure under His enduring promises.

The material things in which I have tried to find security are precarious, but His promises will always remain.

> "Your promises have been throughly tested, and your servant loves them" (Psalms 119: 140).

This is where I can find hope. God's promise for me was enough. As He reminded me of His truth, He had taken me on a journey from anxiety to peace. Because I was courageous enough to answer His question, "What do you want?," He showed me once again He holds all the answers I need.

False Friends: Fear, Manipulation & Control

When our trust has been repeatedly broken in foundational relationships, it can feel vulnerable to expose our deepest needs. We may have even lost touch with them because somewhere along the way, we learned that our needs weren't important.

Rather than risk their exposure and the possibility of our needs being unfulfilled, we may take matters into our own hands and resort to using manipulation and control. These strategies are false friends and destroy relationships. They are ineffective means to satisfying our needs that are rooted in fear.

In her book *The Happy Intercessor,* Beni Johnson says, "All the devil has to do is make sure that we walk in fear; then all of our responses will be out of that place of fear. The most repeated command in the Bible is 'Do not fear'."

"Do not fret—it leads only to evil" (Psalms 37:8).

Fretting is worrying and being anxious. Therefore, fear is a doorway to all sorts of evil. Once we agree with what fear is speaking over our lives, we give fear authority to invite in other forms of evil as well.

For years, I resorted to using manipulation and control to get my needs met. Rather than directly communicating what I needed, I'd subtly hint and set people up to fulfill my desires.

A few months ago, my husband confronted me about feeling manipulated. I had made a comment in front of friends in hopes of persuading Eric to agree with my viewpoint. I was trying to harness the power of peer pressure to convince Eric to do things my way. Obviously, this did not make him feel loved.

At first, when Eric confronted me, I denied it. I felt defensive. That was my old coping mechanism. I had put those ways behind me. Then, I thought I'd better ask Holy Spirit. I simply prayed, "Was I manipulating Eric?" Deep in my heart, the answer came—yes. After renouncing the spirit of manipulation and control and experiencing deeper inner healing a few years ago, I wondered how this spirit had made its way back into my life again.

Then, the Lord graciously revealed the pathway to me: It was because I had partnered with another spirit, the spirit of fear.

Around that time, I had a mole removed and had been worrying about the biopsy. I was listening to the fear of death. I had opened the door a crack and it had pushed its way in with

connection point
Freedom from Fear

What we believe, we empower.[1]

When we believe fear's lies, fear is what rules and reigns in that area of our life. Often, once we let fear into one area of our life, like a weed, it spreads into other areas as well.

We don't want to kick fear out and leave ourselves empty. It's crucial to replace fear with God's presence instead.

> "When an impure spirit comes out of a person, it goes through arid places seeking rest and does not find it. Then it says, 'I will return to the house I left.' When it arrives, it finds the house swept clean and put in order. Then it goes and takes seven other spirits more wicked than itself, and they go in and live there. And the final condition of that person is worse than the first" (Luke 11: 24-26).

Freedom from Fear in Action

Step 1: Renounce (give up) fear and break your partnership with it using this power-packed prayer of repentance.

Pray: "Jesus I confess I have believed fear's lies. I renounce the lie that (name the lie). In the name of Jesus, I break any partnership I've formed with fear and this lie through my thoughts, attitudes, words, or actions, known or unknown. Wash me with your blood. I turn away from fear and I receive Your faith. I choose to believe the truth."

Step 2: Believe the truth.

Ask, "What is the truth You want me to know instead?" Listen. Record what He tells you in your journal.

God is Truth.[2] Asking God to reveal His truth to you is like asking God to reveal Himself. Take hold of the truth. Get it into your life. To assist you, see Connection Point: Making Declarations p. 28.

Step 3: Whenever fear comes back and taunts you with the lie, hold up this truth and put your faith in what God says rather than in what fear says.

When you do this, you're using your shield of faith. Your faith in God's truth will help guard your life and prevent fear's re-entrance.

---

1. Proverbs 18:21
2. John 14:6

"In addition to all this, take up the shield of faith, with which you can extinguish all the flaming arrows of the evil one" (Ephesians 6:16).

The enemy has no real power. However, it can feel scary to see flaming arrows coming your way. Faith is your offensive and defensive weapon for eradicating the assignment of the enemy in your life.

In my own life, I've had to deal with fear on a few levels. The prayer in step 1 is a tool I use in my daily life to "take every thought captive and make it obedient to Christ" (2 Corinthians 10:5). I use it to maintain a fear-free life. It's a weapon for breaking the "habit" or stronghold of fear, worry, and anxiety.

However, I have also experienced deliverance from the spirit of fear when other people have prayed for me and I have actually felt the demonic presence leave. It was a familiar spirit, passed down to me generationally (See Connection Point: Freedom from Generational Sin p. 41).

In fact, after it left, I realized I had never known before what it was like to live without constant fear and anxiety. I didn't know how entrenched it had been in my life. The prayer of deliverance I had received brought forth an instant and miraculous change within me.

If you need deliverance, don't wait! Seek out your church's inner healing ministry or local Sozo ministry (see page 70). God wants you to be truly free! He purchased your freedom on the cross. It's yours for the taking!

"If the son sets you free, you will be free indeed" (John 8:36).

full force. Subsequently, I felt beaten down and powerless.

However, I knew better than to listen to fear. So instead of facing the fact, I denied it. I candy-coated fear with faith and pretended it wasn't there.

At the same time, one of my sons was struggling with reoccurring stomach pains. All the anxiety I had stuffed inside me began to resurface over my son's

I candy-coated fear with faith and pretended it wasn't there

health and I was gripped with fear. It was Sunday morning when things came to a head. I was worshiping God and my lips were quivering. I was on the brink of tears.

I closed my eyes and tried to invite God into the storm inside. I was telling Him all about my son and how worried I was about him. In the midst of my blubbering, God spoke to my heart: "It isn't your son you're so worried about. You're afraid you have cancer and you're going to die. That's what's really going on inside."

The truth hit me hard and opened my heart up before Him. I could finally see. He knew me better than I knew myself. He really knew me, even the yucky parts. Still, He loved and accepted me. He wanted to set me free.

He knew me better than I knew myself

Later, I sought out a dear friend who prayed with me. I realized I had opened the door of my heart to fear and it had also brought with it manipulation and control. I confessed my partnership with fear's plan for my life and repented.

Amazingly, saying no to fear and uprooting its stronghold in my life also meant I was saying no to its friends—manipulation and control. Once again, by the blood of Jesus, I was free!

"The Lord is trustworthy in all he promises and faithful in all he does" (Psalms 145:13).

God is 100 percent faithful and 100 percent trustworthy. Sharing your deepest needs with Him and experiencing His fulfillment of them is a great place to start your healing journey. Like me, if you've been used to finding security in control, even trusting a good and faithful God feels stretching. You're not in charge and it still feels vulnerable.

However, with God's invitation to bring Him your needs, you face a crossroad. You can continue in fear and join with manipulation and control to get your needs met, even though they do a poor job of completely satisfying your core desires.

Or, you can learn to live the way God designed—in trust and interdependence where you take responsibility to know your own heart enough to express it honestly and rely on God and others to help you meet your deep needs.

This is an important step to take as it leads to greater intimacy in our relationships. In the book *Keep Your Love On*, Danny Silk teaches about five levels of communication spanning from the superficial to the intimate. We reach the fifth and most profound level when we're able to talk about what we need. With an awareness of what is going on inside of us and the willingness to share it respectfully, we can cultivate deep intimacy in our most treasured relationships.

For me, this has as been a transformational paradigm shift and a choice I've learned to intentionally make again and again.

Has fear moved in and made a home in your life? Are you ready to kick it out along with anything it's brought with it and live the way God designed you to live—in transparency, freedom, and fulfillment?

Self-Discovery Questions

1. What brings me to my quiet time? Is it obligation or relationship? Be honest.

2. Have I been a slave to fear rather than free to own my core desires and bring them to Jesus? If yes, repent using Connection Point: Freedom from Fear p. 100.

3. Why do I come? What do I really want? More than checking off the quiet time box on my to-do list, what are some of the desires of my heart I am in need of today? List them.

Then, Ask yourself, "What will __(name the desire) give me?" The purpose here is to get to the root of your desire. Determine which core desire does your initial desire indicate? To assist you, see Connection Point: Identifying Your Core Desires p. 96.

Ask Holy Spirit Questions

1. How do You want to meet my need for ____(name the core desire(s) you listed) today?

    He wants to validate your need. Respond to His answer. Put one hand on your heart and hold out your other hand to receive it. Thank and praise Him for meeting your need today.

    Whenever this need rises up in you, return to this place with Papa God. Remind your spirit of His answer and look to Him to continue to meet your need.

2. What else do you have waiting for me as I come?

Pray

"You search me and You know me. You know my every thought. Thank You God for knowing and validating my core desires and deepest needs. I desperately need You to meet these today. I won't look anywhere else. You created me to be most truly satisfied in You alone. I choose to put my hope and trust in You. Come Holy Spirit!"[4]

Declarations

*   When I come to Jesus, He satisfies my deepest needs and desires.[5]

*   I am a good receiver. I open wide my heart and God fills it.[6]

---

4. Psalms 139; Psalms 63:5; Psalms 145:16
5. Psalms 103:4-5; Philippians 4:19
6. Psalms 81:10; Psalms 24:5-10

Step Into Freedom
Choose to do at least one this week.

CREATE A COLLAGE OR PINTEREST BOARD

This exercise will help you draw out your core desires so you can better know yourself and take those desires to Jesus!

Gather a few magazines or jump on Pinterest.com and gather about eight to ten images you really like or find beautiful. They can be anything of your choosing—fashion, home decor, quotes, landscapes, travel destinations, etc.

A Pinterest board is quick and practical. If it makes you more comfortable, you can always make your board "secret." Under the title of the pin, list feelings and words that come to mind as you view the image. You can view an example of my Core Desire Pinterest board at pinterest.com/snmothering/my-core-desire-collage/

If you are able to do a hands-on collage, I highly recommend it. I have found the tactile process to be very healing. Perhaps because the cutting, pasting, and writing take more time than clicking, allowing more space for pondering the images and discovering your own heart.

Have fun spontaneously responding to these images with your spirit. See if you can distinguish which core desire each picture represents for you. Pay attention to the emotions each image is stirring within you.

STEP 1: *Ask yourself: "How do I feel when I look at the picture?*

For example, if you feel calm, then refer to the core desire list p. 95. Which core desire does your feeling of calm most identify with? Peace? Comfort? Security? Goodness?

STEP 2: *Label each image.*

If you are creating a collage in your Quiet Time Journal

or on paper, write the core desire next to each image. If you are using a Pinterest board, type it under the image.

STEP 3: Reflect on the following questions once your collage is complete.

- Which core desire seems to surface the most in my collage?

- Does this surprise me ? Why or why not?

STEP 4: Go back to Ask Holy Spirit Question 1 and ask Him, "How do You want to meet my need for_____(name the most frequent core desire)?"

If you have more than one, by all means, take time to process through each prominent core desire with Holy Spirit. Remember, there are no right or wrong answers.

MAKE DECLARATIONS ABOUT YOUR CORE DESIRES

Making declarations is a way to retrain our spirits to respond with faith rather than fear.

Once you've identified your core desires (Self-Discovery Question 3) and asked how God wants to meet your need (Ask Holy Spirit Question 1), turn these answers into declarations. It might also be helpful to think about when your core desire is especially apparent. Your declarations with these core desires will serve as a reminder to you to turn to Jesus to meet your deep needs during those times.

For example, when I'm doing our family's book-keeping, my core desire for security and for God to come through is most felt. Therefore, my declaration could be, "God will come through for our family when we face financial challenges. He is my security and with Him, I cannot be shaken."

connection point
The Gift of Tongues

At times, you may need Holy Spirit to reveal to you exactly what's going on inside of you. So, simply ask Him, "Holy Spirit, what do I need?" The gift of tongues can help.

Paul is clear. The gift of tongues is for the individual.

"Anyone who speaks in a tongue edifies *themselves*" (1 Corinthians 14:4, emphasis mine).

To edify means to instruct or benefit, especially morally or spiritually; uplift.[1]

The spiritual gift of tongues uplifts and strengthens my spirit and I couldn't live without it.

"For anyone who speaks in a tongue does not speak to people but to God. Indeed, no one understands them; they utter mysteries by the Spirit" (1 Corinthians 14:2).

Praying in tongues provides me an instant connection to God's Spirit. It reveals to me God's heart and my own. If your own heart sometimes proves to be a mystery, this gift can help unveil it to you through God's Spirit.

I'm especially prompted to pray in tongues when I don't know what to pray, I can't put words to what is going on inside, or I feel an urgency to do battle in prayer. It equips me to "utter mysteries by the Spirit" and pray more precise, effective prayers, even if I'm not fully aware of what I'm praying. Even so, as I do, the Bible promises His Spirit is instructing my spirit.

I'll also pray quietly in tongues as I pray for someone else. It's a proactive and instantaneous way for me to get in tune with God's Spirit. It's really His Spirit praying through me. So, I then sense what to do or how to pray in English.

Praying in tongues is a gift of the Holy Spirit.[2] Just as you did when you received the baptism of the Holy Spirit, you can ask the Father for this gift.

Use the prayer from the Connection Point: Baptism of the Holy Spirit p. 64 to help you.

1. Edify. Dictionary.com
2. 1 Corinthians 12:7-11

This is powerful because rather than looking to money as my place of security, I am choosing to agree with God's ability to come through for us and provide as well as with His promise to be my rock in Psalms 62:2. (See Week Three: Step into Freedom for tips on how to recall these declarations throughout your day.)

PERSONALIZE & PRAY PSALMS 139

Using the Quiet Time Method on page 121, read Psalms 139 aloud. I recommend reading it in the Message Bible but any version will do. Don't rush through. Take time to really hear and receive Papa God's care, His purposeful design, His deep knowing of you.

Next, choose one verse. Write it on a note card. Make it a part of your ongoing conversation with Jesus today. Add your own thoughts, praise, or questions to it. Declare its truth over your spirit.

Journal

What did you learn? In your Quiet Time Journal, write about any unexpected core desires you uncovered and how the process of recognizing them is affecting you.

six

Meeting God in Your Secret Place

Constant communion with God is the way of life we are after. When God gets inside of us, we talk about Him and with Him from morning until night, not just during our quiet time.

> "Write these commandments that I've given you today on your hearts. Get them inside of you and then get them inside your children. Talk about them wherever you are, sitting at home or walking in the street; talk about them from the time you get up in the morning to when you fall into bed at night. Tie them on your hands and foreheads as a reminder; inscribe them on the doorposts of your homes and on your city gates" (Deuteronomy 6:7-9, MSG).

Hopefully, like in these verses, over the past few weeks you've been enjoying an increased awareness of God's presence throughout your day.

In addition to this moment by moment connection, Jesus also models for us getting away to a secret place to spend exclusive time with the Father.

"But the news about Him was spreading farther, and large crowds kept gathering to hear Him and to be healed of their illnesses. But Jesus Himself would often slip away to the wilderness and pray [in seclusion]" (Luke 5:15-16, AMP).

Jesus was busy. People were frequently seeking His attention. Okay, He wasn't nursing a baby, shuttling kids to activities, or working through life's challenges with His teenager, but He understood what it was like to be in demand just like us.

In the midst of the hustle and bustle of His demanding life, Jesus knew the value and the indispensability of getting away to spend time with His Papa. He knew that it would refuel Him like nothing else and it was everything to Him. As a mom surrounded by little people all day, you don't have to twist my arm to spend some time alone. Going some place to be alone and pray doesn't sound like a burden but a little slice of paradise. Sometimes, it's not so much the desire to spend time with Jesus we lack but the practical means to do so.

Finding Your Secret Place

Like I said before, God does meet me in the bathroom. In our busy household, there must be a gateway to heaven in this room because it's often where I hear God speak to me. Obviously, it's not so much the sacredness of the place. Most likely, it's the quiet and time in there I use to get in touch with God. It is easier for me to hear and process things with the Lord in the shower.

Susanna Wesley, the mother of nineteen children, including John and Charles Wesley, leaders of the Methodist movement, is told to have found her secret place under her apron. She would be sitting at the table and suddenly throw her apron up over her head. Her children knew mom was meeting with God under there and shouldn't be disturbed.

The bathroom or even an apron can be especially helpful in those more intense seasons of motherhood when both quiet and time are in short supply.

These spontaneous places of encounter with God are a practical lifeline for a busy mom. God is ever-present and can meet us anywhere! This practice of connecting with God in various places and circumstances is part of maturing in Him.

Our Secret Place Set Apart

As we are able, it is also vital we intentionally find a place where we frequently meet with God. It could be a chair, a corner, or a window that is set apart from the rest of the house—a sacred place to us.

In one house we rented, I had a writing desk where I met Jesus. My Bible and other devotionals were there along with fresh flowers for a touch of beauty. With God's help, I was able to carve out a special place that belonged just to the two of us.

A place where I wrote, dreamed, strategized, read, prayed, worshiped, and studied God's Word. Even the sight of my desk, as I passed it during the day, stirred up a longing in my heart to come away and just be with Him.

We are homemakers and so is Jesus. He has gone ahead of us to prepare a place for each of us in heaven.

> "My Father's house has many rooms; if that were not so, would I have told you that I am going there to prepare a place for you?" (John 14:2).

Have you ever wondered what it will look like? One morning, the kids and I were discussing heaven around the breakfast table. We began dreaming about what each of our special places Jesus was preparing for us might look like. Caleb's house (age ten) was all trampolines and a ninja fortress. Joseph's (age eight) was underwater with all his favorite marine animals within reach. While Camille's house (age three) was made of pink bricks.

What I loved about their pictures is how each place reflected their uniqueness, passions, and personalities. Don't you think Jesus celebrates this about each of us too?

Whether this is the way heaven will look I cannot say. Yet, it reminds me our Father goes ahead of me and prepares an exclusive place in His house just for me. The secret place I've prepared for Him in my own home is a space set apart for my communion with God that reflects my uniqueness, passion, and personality.

Coming to the same place at roughly the same time creates a well-worn pathway to His presence

Currently, my place in our living room on our second-hand green couch next to my white, shabby-chic coffee table. My Bible, books, and journal are tucked in a side table waiting for me to pull them out each morning. It's my favorite room, filled with pretty treasures on our fireplace mantle and creamy drapes with soft yellow circles.

You could stop by for a cup of tea and not ever know you were sipping Tetley in my secret place. Still, I know. When I see it in the early morning shadows before the sun rises, it beckons me. It calls to me to come, sit, and be still. My secret place holds expectancy because God and I have made memories there together. If He meets me there regularly, surely He'll come again. And so will I.

It's our space. True, I share it with company, book readers, wrestling boys, and sleepy girls. But in those early hours, it's just ours—mine and Jesus's.

Your secret place may look different from one season to the next. You move houses, babies are born, kids go off to school, furniture gets rearranged. Whatever its shape or size, one thing remains—it's your exclusive place to connect with God.

Each time we come, it's like we form a "spiritual" muscle memory, meaning, "when a movement is repeated over time, a long-term muscle memory is created for that task, eventually allowing it to be performed without conscious effort. This process decreases the need for attention and creates maximum efficiency within the motor and memory systems."[1]

Our secret place provides a space where we build our track record with God and make history together. It's a time and place where we encounter the Living Lord Jesus again and again. Coming to the same place at roughly the same time creates a well-worn pathway to His presence. Because we're repeating this practice over time, it takes less effort and becomes more satisfying. It isn't the only path we'll take to meet God but it's one we can intentionally cultivate day after day.

What's Your Sweet Spot?

"From here on, worshiping the Father will not be a matter of the right place but with the right heart" (John 4:23, TPT).

Your secret place can be a particular space in your home, but it also can be found in activities you enjoy. After all, it's essentially about engaging our heart with His. Any moment in time or any place where we regularly encounter God's presence becomes our secret place.

While I especially meet God in the creative, heart-felt process of writing, my husband comes alive to God in nature.

---

1. En.wikipedia.org/wiki/muscle_memory

He's a former river raft and kayak guide. He even experienced the baptism of the Holy Spirit on a river in France. He'll hike for miles and feel God's presence.

I'm too nervous to hike for miles (and too worn out), fearful of a run-in with a moose (while that might seem outlandish, it was a real threat when we lived in Alaska), or someone hiding in the bushes waiting to attack me.

It took my husband and I a while to understand that the ways we connect with God are different, yet equally powerful.

Dr. Myra Perrine, in her book *What's Your God Language?*, points out "that greater spiritual passion resulted when people were pursuing God in ways they enjoyed and found most life-giving. Often these spiritual preferences were not given expression; instead, people seemed to be doing what they were taught to do, almost afraid of what they enjoyed. When this occurred, I noticed that spiritual satisfaction declined, as did a person's sense of closeness to God."[2]

Most of my Christian life, I had been trying to use a quiet time model that didn't particularly feed my spirit or my sense of closeness to God. It was highly structured and hard to achieve.

Today, I feel the most spiritually satisfied when God and I are writing, learning, or creating together. I used to feel guilty writing first thing in the morning instead of having a traditional quiet time.

Now, in addition to reading my Bible, I'm learning to invite Him into my writing and enjoy God's presence while we spend time doing this together.

Whether your way of connecting with God is in nature, serving others, solitude, or the intellectual (to name just a few), God has designed you with a particular "spiritual temperament."

2. Myra Perrine, *What's Your God Language?: Connecting with God through Your Unique Spiritual Temperament,* 2007.

Discovering this temperament will help you connect more deeply with God and feel more spiritually alive. Dr. Gary Thomas, the originator of the spiritual temperament concept, has defined the following nine tendencies we have for drawing closer to God.[3]

- The Activist
- The Ascetic
- The Caregiver
- The Contemplative
- The Enthusiast
- The Intellectual
- The Naturalist
- The Sensate
- The Traditionalist

So, how do you discover your spiritual temperament? Listen to your life. Defining your spiritual temperament is really about knowing and accepting yourself.

What makes you tick? What do you do to feel closest to God? Where do you feel most spiritually alive?[4]

This journey of self-discovery must also be one of self-acceptance. You're probably familiar with the expression, "You can't put a square peg in a round hole." This can be applied to our spiritual temperaments as well. You can't force a naturalist to connect with God the way an intellectual would. Nor can you turn an activist into a contemplative.

Defining your spiritual temperament is really about knowing and accepting yourself

Any personal assessment we make is intended only to help us lean into our natural bent rather than confine us to it. We may be tempted to compare ourselves with others. We

3. For a more detailed description, go to Dr. Gary Thomas's article for Focus on the Family at thrivingfamily.com/Features/Magazine/2011/nine-spiritual-temperaments

4. To more exactly categorize yourself, take the spiritual temperament quiz at thrivingfamily.com/Features/Web/2011/your-spiritual-temperament-quiz

might align ourselves with one particular spiritual temperament and then envy another's. On the contrary, we should celebrate our own uniqueness rather than try to change it to look like someone else's. The way we meet God, experience His presence, and satisfy our spirits can be found in unique places and ways because God has made each of us unique. You are being conformed to God's image, not someone else's, and He likes the way He made you![5]

So rather than fight it, embrace it! Get to know your distinct spiritual bent and go with it. In fact, Dr. Myra Perrine describes our spiritual temperament as a gift to God: "It is how you best express love to Him and where your passion for Him is stirred. God derives pleasure as we love Him and receive His love and the way He made us is the way He knows we will most readily find our joy and delight in Him."

Eric Liddell, whose story is depicted in the famous movie *Chariots of Fire*, is an example of a man who knew and accepted how He best experienced God. He was a missionary to China and an Olympic gold-medalist of the 400-meter dash. His sister tried to persuade him to give up running along with his Olympic dream so he could get on with his more "spiritual work" as a missionary. But Liddell is quoted to have responded, "I believe God made me for a purpose, but he also made me fast. And when I run I feel His pleasure." Along with missionary work, running had become a place where he experienced God. It was his spiritual act of worship.

> "Therefore, brothers, by the mercies of God, I urge you to present your bodies as a living sacrifice, holy and pleasing to God; this is your spiritual worship" (Romans 12:1).

He had found his sweet spot. Make sure you find yours too.

---

5. Romans 8:29

The Best is Yet to Come

In the Gospel of John, Jesus is introduced to Nathanael who is skeptical that Jesus is truly the Messiah. Upon meeting him, Jesus tells Nathanael He saw him sitting under the shade of a fig tree. Nathanael is absolutely floored. In his astonishment, he declares Jesus to be the Son of God and the King of Israel. Jesus replies,

> "Do you believe simply because I told you I saw you sitting under a fig tree? You will experience even more impressive things than that. I prophesy to you eternal truth: From now on you will see an open heaven and gaze upon the Son of Man" (John 1:50-51, TPT).

Nathanael has an amazing encounter with the living Lord Jesus and Holy Spirit reveals to him that Jesus is indeed the Messiah. But Jesus doesn't stop there. He promises Nathanael more.

It's like He's saying to Nathanael and to you and me, "This is only the beginning, my child. I want to reveal myself to you. Anything that has been in our way (old mind-sets, doubt, fear, lies, confusion, even your quiet time) will be leveled and I will open up the way so there is nothing between you and Me. My desire is that you and I spend time together unhindered and in complete intimacy."

Just as Jesus did, I want to prophesy over you that from now on, you will see an open heaven and gaze upon Jesus face to face. You have encountered Him before, but the best is yet to come. Keep expecting. Keep hoping. Take time to meet Him in your secret places!

> "I will give you hidden treasures, riches stored in secret places, so that you may know that I am the Lord, the God of Israel, who summons you by name" (Isaiah 45:3).

Come to the secret place, receive hidden treasures stored up for you, and spend time with Jesus so that you may know, intimately and personally, the one who calls you by name and says, "You are mine!"[6]

Self-Discovery Questions

1. What kinds of places (in or out of my home) do I spontaneously meet with God?

2. Have I created a place to intentionally meet with God? If so, why is it special to me? If not, where in my home can I devote a space to grow our relationship?

   Think about what you'll put in your secret place or how you'll arrange it to set it apart from the rest of your home (decor, resources, pictures, etc.).

3. What's my sweet spot? In which activities do I especially experience God's pleasure?

4. Which spiritual temperament do I most identify with?

Ask Holy Spirit Questions

1. How have You uniquely designed me to personally connect with Your presence? How am I wired to especially experience the pleasure of being with you?

2. What do You have waiting for me in our secret places? Ask Him for a picture. Draw it in your journal or describe it.

3. Is there anything hindering me from experiencing true intimacy with You? If so, what is it? If necessary, take a moment to repent of any sin, forgive, or break

---

6. Isaiah 43:1

agreement with a lie you've been believing. Give Jesus any hindrances. (See Quick Reference: Connection Point Exchanging Truth for Lies p. 71.)

Pray

"Thank You Jesus that You created me for Yourself. Help me understand and accept the unique way You designed me to connect with You. I receive everything You have waiting for me. I want to feel spiritually alive! I believe the best is yet to come!"[7]

Declarations

- God has treasure hidden for me in secret places. He lovingly leads me to it and I discover and receive His riches.[8]

- In my quiet times, because of the cross, I experience an open heaven and meet with Jesus face to face.[9]

Step into Freedom

Choose to do at least one this week.

HAVE FUN WITH GOD

Purpose this week to spend time with God in a way you really enjoy. Try connecting with Him as you participate in one of your favorite activities (dancing, painting, hiking, sitting, singing, reading, sewing, being with your kids, etc.).

START CREATING YOUR SECRET PLACE

Pick a place in your home or yard where you will intentionally go to experience God's presence and hear His voice. Set it apart with a few special mementos of Jesus and your encounters with Him. Add any Quiet Time crafts you've created!

---

7. John 1:50-51; Isaiah 45:3; Psalms 139:14
8. Isaiah 40:11; Isaiah 45:3
9. Deuteronomy 34:10; John 1:50-51

TRY A NEW QUIET TIME METHOD

In your secret place, do one or two of the Quiet Time Methods suggested p. 121 to 126. Try one on for size. You may end up adopting one of these methods into your regular quiet times or deciding it's simply not the best fit for you.

Once again, we're seeking to keep things in our relationship with Jesus fresh. Like in marriage, commitment and routine help us be intentional about building our relationship. Yet, if it's only about commitment and routine, the relationship looses its excitement. Mixing up the ways we connect with God keeps our interaction with Him spontaneous and full of adventure!

Journal

What did you learn? In your Quiet Time Journal, write what you are most excited about as you connect with God in new ways and places this week.

Quiet Time Methods
Nurturing Your Intimate Connection with Jesus

Once I broke free from my restrictive quiet time box, I was nervous about using any method for fear that I'd find myself back in shackles again. The reality is, it isn't the methods that had brought me into bondage, rather it was my mind-sets. It was the lies I had believed about myself and God. Once I experienced healing from my past and made it a regular practice, I was free to live fully in constant connection with Jesus throughout the day and during the time I set aside to seek Him.

A quiet time is all about seeking His face—His presence. I wanted to share with you a handful of quiet time methods I've enjoyed because they connect me with the person of Jesus and His presence, rather than just helping me learn about Him.

By no means is it exhaustive. I only wanted to perhaps offer you some new options so you can walk into freedom while intentionally pressing into Jesus.

Any method can become about performance if we don't deal with any pain or lies in our own hearts. Keep seeking authenticity with yourself and with Jesus. He will lead you to freedom because that is what He came to do. He came to set the captives free.[1]

---

1. Isaiah 61:1

S.H.A.P.E.D.[2]

This acronym stands for Scripture, Hear, Apply, Pray, Exalt, Declare. My favorite part of using this method is the "H" for hear. This method is purposeful about approaching the Scriptures ready to hear God speak to us. Below, you'll find the suggested format.

However, I often skip around. For example, I'll read Scripture, pray, hear, exalt, apply and declare. Or I'll read Scripture, exalt, hear, declare, apply, and pray. My point is: it doesn't matter how you do it, just get the conversation with Jesus going.

The Scriptures feel so much more alive when we start interacting with Him. Hear His voice and respond. There's nothing like it! Here's how it works:

- (S) Scripture: Choose a small section of Scripture (five to ten verses). Write down or underline certain words or phrases God highlights to you.

- (H) Hear: In your journal, write "My daughter whom I love, today I want to tell you..." Then sit and listen. What is He speaking to you about what you just read?

- (A) Apply: Ask God what He wants you to do as a result of what you've read. Write down any action steps you will take.

- (P) Pray: Pour out your heart and respond to Him and His love for you. Ask for help, thank Him, ask Him more questions (whatever comes to mind).

- (E) Exalt: Praise God for who He is and for what He is going to do in your life.

- (D) Declare: Turn what you heard God say in the (H) section into a brief declaration over your life (one to two sentences).

---

2. Adapted from Pastor Fred Leonard of Mountain View Community Church in Fresno, California, Mountainview.org.

Ten and Ten

I once heard Kris Vallotton speak about the importance of spending time daily with the Lord. For those short on time, he recommended spending ten minutes listening after asking, "What do you want to talk to me about today, Jesus?" and ten minutes reading the Bible.

Jesus speaks through Holy Spirit to our own hearts and through reading His Word. While listening, you might try journaling. You may find you begin with your own thoughts. As you go along, tucked in will be some of Holy Spirit's truth and wisdom too. You may have to comb through it for gold, but you'll soon recognize His voice between the lines.

I love how Havilah Cunnington puts it, "Even when I can't hear God, I can still find Him in the Word." We want to live a life in continual pursuit of His presence. He is our greatest treasure. We can find Him in many places in our lives and we are blessed with the Bible where He consistently shows up! When we go through a season when it seems difficult to hear Him speaking to us, the Bible becomes that changeless place where we can always encounter His truth and love for us.

Personalize & Pray Scripture

We can't read the Word like it was written for someone else. His Word is timeless, alive, and active! This method helps us hear the Scriptures like a love letter, written just for us.

Make it about you and God by personalizing Scripture. For example, pick a verse. Insert your name, she, I, me, we, or us. For example, "For You know the plans You have for (Ashley)," declares the Lord, "plans to prosper (me) and not to harm (me), plans to give (me) hope and a future" (Jeremiah 29:11).

Turn the verse into a prayer and declaration over your life or someone else's.

Meditate and Dialogue Through Scripture[3]

This is a beautiful way to interact with God's Word through a dialogue of prayer. It involves thanksgiving, revelation, obedience, and empowerment. So many goodies packed into this one method!

STEP 1: Pick a passage from the Bible. Thank God for a particular truth within those verses.

> I like reading a portion of Scripture and underlining the verse or verses that tug at my heart, fascinate, or intrigue me. For example, when reading Song of Songs 2, you might underline "I am at rest in this love" (Song of Songs 2:6). You could pray, "Thank you Jesus that I can be at rest in Your love."

STEP 2: Ask God for a deeper understanding of the truth. In doing so, we are asking for revelation and for Him to teach us more about this truth.[4]

> For example, using again the above verse, you could pray, "Show me how to rest in Your love."
>
> Or when reading, "And run with me to the higher place" (Song of Songs 2:13, TPT), ask God, "Show me what's in the higher place and why You're inviting me there?"

STEP 3: Commit to obey God's word. Express your desire to Him.

> For example, using Song of Songs 2:13, you could pray, "I will run away with you to the higher place. It will be my passion and the focus of my day."

---

3. Adapted from Mike Bickle's online teaching on the Song of Solomon
4. Ephesians 1:17

STEP 4: Ask Holy Spirit to empower you to obey.

We know Holy Spirit gives us power to choose righteous living. We are no longer governed by sin but God's Holy Spirit within us.[5]

For example, again using the above verse, you could pray, "Holy Spirit, help me to run to Jesus when He woos me. Help me to drop everything and simply come."

Use Various Translations

Reading a Scripture passage in a variety of translations keeps well-known verses from feeling stale so you can hear God speaking to you afresh! My favorite translations are The New Living, The Amplified Bible, The Message, and The Passion Translation. These translations tend to use today's language and feel more conversational to me. Whatever your preference, choose translations that keep God's Word feeling alive to you!

Soak in His Presence with Your Kids

Bring your kids along with you on this journey. It's powerful to model intimate connection with Jesus and introduce your kids to Him in this personal way. I started doing this during a very intense season of motherhood. I had five kids under the age of six which included twin baby boys! Yikes! Modeling was just a by-product of a mama desperate to find Jesus in her all-consuming world.

To "soak," put on worship music and sit or lie down to receive and rest in Him. The kids can join in the room, sometimes on a pillow (to help define their own personal space), sometimes

5. Romans 6:14-22

drawing what Jesus is showing them, and sometimes simply playing quietly. It's one way of carving out some intentional connection time with Jesus when it seems impossible to get away alone with Him.

Bible Studies & Devotionals

Supernatural Mothering: Where God's Presence and Power Invade Motherhood by Ashley Brendle

My twelve-week study focuses on getting the dialogue going with God. It's full of questions for Holy Spirit so you can practice hearing His voice more readily and believing the truth of who He is and who you are as a mother. This study helps you break out of old habits into new, life-giving ways of relating to God and your kids!

Jesus Calling: Enjoying Peace in His Presence by Sarah Young

Each day in this best-selling devotional is written as if Jesus Himself is speaking to you personally. I like to look up the Scriptures Young cites for each day's entry to deepen my encounter with His message for me.

Encountering Jesus in the Song of Songs by Mike Bickle

This is a free video series that takes you through the Song of Songs.[1] It will help you understand how God sees you and how He feels about you. Song of Songs is a revelation of God's affection for us. If you've been curious about this book of the Bible but felt it was difficult to decode, Mike Bickle's teaching will help you unlock it!

Questions for Jesus: Conversational Prayer Around Your Deepest Desires by Tony Stolzfus

When I get in tune with my core desires, I use this book to help me let Jesus speak into my deepest needs. There are fifty-two meditations, each one focused on the various core desires listed p. 95. My favorite part is the questions for Jesus listed at the end of each meditation. They are crafted to help us hear God's answers so we can get each core desire perfectly met in Jesus.

The Seven Longings of the Human Heart by Mike Bickle

To understand more about your God-given needs and longings, you'll want to access this free teaching by Mike Bickle.[2] It validates and affirms these longings God purposefully created us with to draw us to Himself. This thorough teaching has study notes you can download to use with the video.

---

1. mikebickle.org/resources/category/intimacy/song-of-songs/
2. mikebickle.org/resources/resource/3657

Quiet Time Declarations

1. I am God's precious daughter, dearly loved. I come today to spend time with Papa. It is from my connection with Him that I live and move and have my being. I position myself wide open under the spout of His mercy and grace (Acts 17:28; Romans 8:14-16; Hebrews 4:16).

2. Because of the cross, I experience constant, intimate connection with God throughout my day. Nothing can stand in the way of me living in His presence (Romans 8:38-39; Hebrews 4:16).

3. God shows me creative ways to establish the necessary boundaries to tend the garden of my heart and prioritize spending time connecting with Him (Psalms 16:6; Revelation 2:4).

4. I guard my heart and the fruit of the Spirit blossoms in it! (Proverbs 4:23; Galatians 5:22-23).

5. My strivings cease when I rest in God's love for me (Song of Songs 2:6; 1 John 4:18).

6. The time I spend with God is rich and abundant. He speaks to me and I hear Him. We share an intimate dialogue that satisfies my soul (Psalms 63:3-5; Psalms 84:10).

7. When I seek after God, I find Him. He rewards my pursuit of Him by giving me more of Himself (Psalms 34:8; Hebrews 11:6).

8. There is no lack in Jesus. Everything He has is mine (Luke 15:31; Psalms 34:10).

9. When I come to Jesus, He satisfies my deepest needs and desires (Psalms 103:4-5; Philippians 4:19).

10. I am a good receiver. I open wide my heart and God fills it (Psalms 81:10; Psalms 24:5-10).

11. God has treasure hidden for me in secret places. He lovingly leads me to it and I discover and receive His riches (Isaiah 40:11; Isaiah 45:3).

12. In my quiet times, because of the cross, I experience an open heaven and meet with Jesus face to face (Deuteronomy 34:10; John 1:50-51).

Quick Reference
Connection Points

Strategies for restoring, maintaining, and deepening your heart to heart connection with God.

Acknowledgments

My husband and children: Thank you for all your love, support, and sacrifice that helped me publish this book. You have taught me so many life lessons. Thank you for investing in me! I love each of you so much!

Amy Beth Beaver: Your editing, graphic design, and formatting have made this book a beautiful work of art. Without your in-depth edits, this book would have lacked the clarity and smooth transitions it now has. Your constant belief in this project and willingness to do whatever it took to get it off the ground was wind beneath my wings. Thank you!

Sarah Jackson: Your willingness to lead a study from a half-finished book blessed me. You wrestled through the rough spots and brought forth the book's value. The Connection Points emerged through your insight. Thank you and Rob for also providing a writing refuge for me at the Daniel House. I'm forever grateful for all your love and support.

Shandon Gerbrandt: Thank you for joining in the book study with your whole heart! Because you thoroughly applied each question and activity, others now have a more refined and powerful way to approach their own journeys through the book. I am so thankful for your suggestions and encouragement.

Liberty Dictson: Whenever I have doubts, I call you! Your belief in me and this book helped keep me going. Thank you for editing and consulting me on the cover. I can't wait to see how God wants to use you to bring this book to young women!

The ECCK Quiet Time Class: You women are brave! Thank you for taking the book as is and joining me on the journey. Your presence every Tuesday was a constant encouragement and I saw your faces as I revised its content. You showed me the gaps in the book and it's now richer because of you.

What would it be like to meet Jesus in the daily grind of motherhood and always have everything you need to thrive as a mother, not just survive?

This twelve-week study will lead you into intimate encounters with Jesus while giving you practical, life-giving tools to sustain His presence and power in your mothering.

Its dynamic components will enable you to hear God's personal message for you in the midst of the hustle and bustle of motherhood.

Weekly Declarations | Real-Life Stories | Scripture Study
Healing Prayers | Action Steps | Journaling

STUDY TOPICS INCLUDE:
- Your Competence is from God
- The Power of Renewing Your Mind
- The Strategic Mother
- Walking in Christ's Authority
- Freedom from Generational Sin
- The Peaceful Mother
- Everything You Need
- A Wise Woman Builds Her House
- Releasing the Kingdom in Your Home
- The Joyful Mother
- The Promised Outpouring

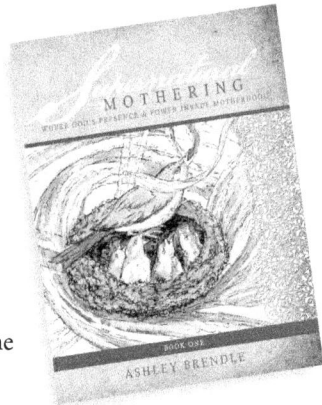

A Leader's Guide for Supernatural Mothering is Available
Do the study independently or gather with other moms in a small group setting and go on this transformational journey together!

For more information or to purchase, go to SupernaturalMothering.com

"Your spirit will soar and you will be changed as you gain Heaven's perspective and the authority to operate in who God has called you to be as a world changing individual, wife, and mother in these last days."

Lori Byrne

Director and Vice President of Nothing Hidden Ministries
Bethel Church, Redding, California

www.ingramcontent.com/pod-product-compliance
Lightning Source LLC
LaVergne TN
LVHW051416080426

835508LV00022B/3105

9780997838305